THE
BA'TH AND SYRIA

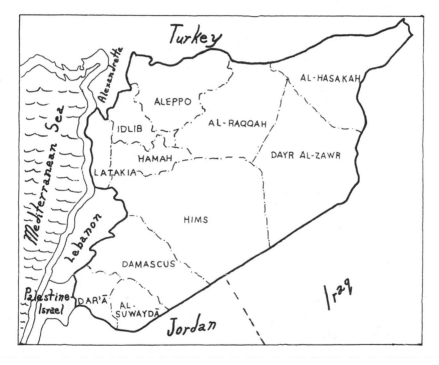

1947~1982

THE KINGSTON PRESS SERIES:

Leaders, Politics and Social Revolution in the Islamic World

Carl Max Kortepeter, General Editor

1. The Ba'th in Syria: The Evolution of Ideology, Party and State (1945-1981) by Robert W. Olson (University of Kentucky)

2. Britain's Withdrawal from the Middle East, 1947-1971: The Economic and Strategic Imperatives by Jacob Abadi (Fairleigh Dickinson University)

3. Ralph Khuri's Channels of the French Revolution to the Arab East Edited by Charles Issawi (Princeton University) and Translated by Ihsan Abbas (American University of Beirut) (Forthcoming)

4. The United States and the Middle East: The Flawed Foundations by C. Max Kortepeter (New York University) (Forthcoming)

5. Atatürk and the Transformation of Turkish Culture Edited by Günsel Renda (Hacettepe University)

6. Hajj Amin al-Husayni, Mufti of Palestine by Taysir Jbara (University of Algeria) (Forthcoming)

7. Nuclear Weapons in the Middle East: Dimensions and Responsibilities by Taysir Nashif (United Nations) (Forthcoming)

THE BA'TH AND SYRIA, 1947 to 1982 THE EVOLUTION OF IDEOLOGY, PARTY, AND STATE

From The French Mandate to the Era of Hafiz al-Asad

Robert W. Olson

THE KINGSTON PRESS, INC.
Princeton, N.J.

Published in the United States of America in 1982
by The Kingston Press, Inc.
P.O. Box 1456, Princeton, N.J. 08540

© 1982 by The Kingston Press, Inc.

ISBN 0-940670-18-6

Printed by Edwards Brothers, Inc.,
Ann Arbor, Michigan 48106

AMANDA AND REBECCA

"Two birds of my heart,
Two lights of my eyes."

TABLE OF CONTENTS

PREFACE

The professor of Middle Eastern studies, teaching largely beginning students, is confronted with two basic kinds of books. One is the survey book which treats the history of the area from 500 A.D. to the present in approximately 400 pages. Ten or fifteen pages are allocated to each major movement, e.g., pan-Islam, pan-Arabism or the history of the Ottoman Empire and ten pages or so cover the history of each country in the area. The second sort of book is the increasingly proliferating political science monograph which emphasizes social change and 'strategies of development.' The last gives short shrift indeed to the political history and the history of institutions which are so essential for beginning students. This literature is placed in the context of the problems of all underdeveloped 'third world' nations and is geared to the advanced student. There is a desperate need for an intermediate essay which combines these two approaches. This is especially true for the student who simply cannot master the theoretical literature of the social science approach, especially the student with an inadequate background in the history and culture of the Middle East. The undergraduate and graduate student and also the interested reader requires a narrative with an interpretation covering a period of twenty to twenty-five years, a longer time span than is usually covered in any detail in most books. There is also a need to include diplomatic history and an interpretation of that history so that it becomes meaningful to the student. This is true especially in the case of Syria where the policies of Israel and of the super powers, especially the policies of the United States, have had an immense impact on the course of Syria's history. I hope my essay will contribute to meeting these needs.

ACKNOWLEDGMENTS

I wish to thank the editors of Oriente Moderno for their permission, and especially Professor Pier Giovanni Donini, to reprint the material which comprises the first seven chapters of this book and which first appeared in volumes LVII and LVIII of Oriente Moderno. I once again wish to thank all of the scholars who contributed to that essay: Professors Raymond Hinnebusch, Iliya Harik, Phebe Marr and Aladdin Hreib who gave me permission to use and to quote from their work. I also wish to thank Professor Carl Max Kortepeter for suggesting the book as it appears here. Serving as an editor of Kingston Press, he has been generous and helpful in seeing the book through publication. The book would not have been written if I had not received generous help from the following scholars: Professor Alasdair Drysdale kindly sent me a copy of his "The Syrian Armed Forces in National Politics: The Role of the Geographic and Ethnic Periphery," which will appear in a forthcoming volume edited by Andrej Korbonski and Roman Kolkowicz entitled Soldiers, Peasants, and Bureaucrats and will be published by Allen and Unwin in 1982. John Devlin kindly sent me three chapters and gave me permission to cite from his forthcoming book tentatively titled, Syria: A Country Profile which will be published by Westview Press in 1982. Professor Ali E. Hillal Dessouki also graciously consented to send me a copy of the book which he is editing about the Islamic resurgent movements in the Middle East which will be published by Praeger in 1982. The article in that book, "The Islamic Movement in Syria: Sectarian Conflict and Urban Rebellion in an Authoritarian Populist Regime," written by Raymond Hinnebusch is the only detailed scholarly work on the 'Islamic' oppositional movement in Syria of which I am aware. Any student who is interested in contemporary Syrian history and politics should consult this work. I wish to express my deep appreciation to all of the above scholars whose work made this book possible.

I want to thank my colleague Paul Forand who graciously took a few days from his spring vacation to proofread the final draft. Max Kortepeter was more than just an editor. He made comments and corrections read and re-read the manuscript. His criticism and corrections have greatly improved the book. My wife also happily agreed to proofread the galleys. Robert Tri and Timothy Ballard translated some difficult passages from German and Arabic for me.

For the transliteration of Arabic I have used an adapted version of the Library of Congress system without diacritical marks for publication purposes. The words Alawite and Alawi are used interchangeably.

Lexington, 14 December, 1981   Robert Olson

INTRODUCTION

Dr. Olson has taken upon himself an important task: to clarify the major political, social and ideological developments in Syria since the close of World War II(1945). The undertaking, which Professor Olson has completed with consumate skill, bears a special significance for British, Canadian, American and indeed all English-reading audiences, for we have not had available a great deal of information about modern Syria. The exceptions to this general rule are the serious studies of Syria by such scholars as Kamil Abu Jabber, John Devlin, Philip Hitti, Albert Hourani and Itamar Rabinovich. By contrast, there are a number of popular and scholarly books available to the French reading public because of the centuries of commercial and political ties between France and the eastern Mediterranean. In this century, the League of Nations after World War I assigned to France the mandates of Syria and Lebanon wherein she remained the dominant political force until 1946.

As long as Syria(mostly included within the province of Damascus) remained within the confines of the Ottoman-Islamic Empire from the years 1516 to 1918, the importance of national identity for Muslim Syrians(especially Sunni or orthodox Muslims) was not a major issue because the Ottoman state favored Sunni Islam. Prior to the twentieth century, the allegiance with which one identified one's self, above that of family and clan, was one's own religious sect, not one's national or imperial government.

But as World War I drew near and as European and American missionaries, commercial activities, and military invasions became more frequent and as young Muslims, Christians and Jews attended western schools, Arab leaders and intellectuals became well-informed and quite interested in western ideologies such as liberalism, nationalism and secularism. It was thus logical that they would seek to establish a new rationale or ideology to better fit the demands of modern life, a new norm which might overcome sectarian parochialism and destructive civil strife. It must be remembered, however, that only a small per cent of Middle Eastern society wished to depart from the strict precepts of Islam and the ways of their traditional communities. Thus, for every new idea put forth by the new intellectuals, a number of arguments in favor of the old ways were strongly supported by traditional groups within Middle Eastern society. This strong competition between traditional and modern lifestyles and ideologies has persisted until the present day and this theme underlies much of what Professor Olson details about modern Syria and the ideological and practical concerns of the Ba'th leadership.

The Young Turks who seized power in Istanbul in 1908 had sought the allegiance of restless provinces such as the province of Damascus (including much of modern Syria and Palestine) by re-establishing the Ottoman constitution and parliament first instituted in 1876. Yet even the Turks called for new elections on the basis of sectarian allegiance and failed to give the Arabs their proportional representation in parliament, thus they kept alive old rivalries and religious sectarian loyalties.

During World War I, following the supression of Arab nationalists by the Ottoman military governor, Jemal Pasha, in Damascus, many Syrians revolted against Ottoman rule and welcomed Faysal, son of Sharif Husayn of Mecca, and the British into Damascus(October 1, 1918).(Those who have seen the film, "Lawrence of Arabia," will remember the taking of Damascus.) The elation of being 'free' from Ottoman Turkish rule was quickly dampened when Faysal was driven out of Damascus by the French General Gouraud on July 24, 1920. The French mandate, in effect, began then.

Initially Syria was divided into four centrally controlled districts: Great Lebanon, Damascus (with Druze Mountain), Aleppo(with Alexandretta) and Latakia (the Alawi territory). Later, Druze Mountain and Alexandretta were also given separate status. Upon the withdrawal of French forces in 1946, a national Syrian government came to power, but the factionalism encouraged by the French remained. Lebanon had become a separate entity in 1926 (reflecting its large Christian population), Turkey had annexed Alexandretta province in 1938 and the remaining districts formed modern Syria. To set up Great Lebanon, France had appended certain Muslim mountain districts of the old Ottoman province of Damascus to Lebanon, a move resented by Syrian nationalists. It is little wonder that Syrian nationalists entered the post World War II era with considerable misgivings about the intentions of the Great Powers, and at the same time, anxious to give their allegiance to an ideology which would stand above the religious sectarianism so often manipulated by the Turks, the French and other Western governments.

One such ideology was the concept of Greater Syria which called for the union of Lebanon, Syria, Iraq and Palestine under the leadership of the Hashemite family. This plan offered a modicum of security to these semi-desert and mountainous regions of low population. (Sharif Husayn of Mecca's family, including his sons, King Abdullah of Jordan and King Faysal of Iraq, gained their legitimacy by tracing their ancestry to the Hashim family of the Prophet Muhammed).

With the establishment of the state of Israel in 1948, another region which had been an integral part of the old Syrian province was torn away with the aid of western powers. Thus the Syrians since World War I had seen great chunks of Syrian territory seized by other states with the aid and protection of western governments. It is not surprising that Ba'thist ideology, advocating a more equitable distribution of the meagre national resources of Syria and a political unity free from sectarian favoritism and nepotism, attracted many adherents in Syria and in other Arab states. True, before accepting Ba'thism wholeheartedly an interlude of union with Nasir's Egypt took place from 1958 to 1961, which must be viewed, in part, as a move to participate in the security of a Pan-Arab entity advocated by Nasir. When the experiment with the United Arab Republic went sour, the Syrians still felt exposed and vulnerable, particularly after the terrible destruction of Syrian towns and the high loss of life in the June, 1967 war with Israel.

Syria was one of the poorest Arab countries, and it had no benefactor to re-supply its army and to rebuild its economy on the scale that the United States provided for Israel or the Soviets for Egypt; moreover, after every war or every expropriation of Palestinian homes and farmlands by Israelis; Syria, Lebanon and Jordan, the poorest countries of the area, were forced to absorb large numbers of Palestinian refugees driven out of Israel.

Simply to break the pattern of economic hardship and incremental annexation, not to be anti-American as many analysts imply, the Syrians accepted a Ba'thist ideology and a closer relationship with the Soviet Union. Syria would have preferred a close relationship with the United States, and still does, but such a relationship was unattainable as long as the United States continued to support Israeli intransigence and expansion into neighboring states.

xvi

This favored relationship of Israel with the United States did not alter in the 1973 war. Syrian troops fought to recover the Golan Heights, occupied by Israel in 1967, but the United States remained silent when the Israelis destroyed the entire Syrian city of Quneitra before returning it to Syria after the Kissinger peace negotiations in 1974. Moreover, the United States remained indifferent when Israel annexed the Golan Heights in 1981. Israel is a jealous lover guarding her special relationship with the United States and taking every opportunity to destroy normal ties between the United States and Arab countries by propaganda within America and by military operations in the Middle East.

Even while this manuscript was passing through the page-proof stage, Israel invaded Lebanon in June of 1982. This attack was aimed at the Palestinian forces which had entrenched themselves in southern Lebanon after being driven out of their homes and farms in Palestine (now Israel) in succeeding wars 1948, 1967 and 1973. The Israelis drew Syria into the present conflict, even though Syrian forces in the Beka'a Valley attempted to remain neutral. Syria had entered Lebanon during the Lebanese civil war of 1976 to establish a cease-fire between the left wing coalition (mostly Muslim) and the rightist coalition (mostly Maronite Christian).

The Israelis invaded Lebanon with a force of roughly 100,000 men in tanks and armored personnel carriers to destroy the Palestinian army of about 15,000. At all times the Israelis had complete air cover which they used to destroy 90 Syrian MIG aircraft and 400 Syrian tanks (Israeli sources)-- heavy losses for a non-beligerent! The Israelis used tactics similar to those used by allied forces during World War II. Rather than commit troops against the well-trained Palestinian forces, they used their aircraft, heavy mortars and artillery to pulverize such cities as Tyre and

Sidon with a considerable loss of life among the civilian population.

The high loss of life has been attributed by most journalists to American weapons supplied to the Israelis on a cost-free basis by the United States Congress and included such civilian killers as cluster bombs and phosphorus shells.

In many respects, the Syrian leadership prepared the way for a Palestinian and Syrian defeat. The Israeli strategy, greatly aided by Egypt's signing of the Camp David agreement, has always been to defeat the Arab states one by one. The government of Syria provided Israel with a golden opportunity to destroy the Palestinian forces in Lebanon by weakening herself internally and alienating her Jordanian, Lebanese and Iraqi neighbors. Apart from these diplomatic lapses on the part of Syria, there were of course difficulties with weapons, training and morale which Dr. Olson's study goes a long way towards explaining.

Even as Dr. Olson has stated, the government of Syria moved in the late seventies from a position of more or less neutrality with regard to sectarian matters to a position which left the impression of a bias in favor of the Alawites. Moreover al-Asad failed to curb reckless elements in his own entourage, notably his brother who headed the shock troops.

The Syrian government indeed showed extreme insensitivity to the graveness of the Israeli challenge to all independent governments in the Middle East when Syria mobilized its troops against Jordan early in the Iraqi-Iranian War and later, when al-Asad declared in favor of Iran.

As to the attack by the Muslim brotherhood on the artillery school in Aleppo in 1979, the murder by an armed group of an Alawi wedding party in Hama in 1981 and the leveling of many parts of Hama by the Syrian army, the condemnation must be the same. Regardless of party or sectarian allegiance, the threat to Syrian independence from Israel has always been so grave that no sectarian group can afford to weaken national unity, whether or not that group happens to be the party in power. (One must not, of course, rule out the possibility that Israel, the Maronite faction in Lebanon or indeed other Middle Eastern governments helped engineer some of the assaults in Syria which have been attributed to the Muslim brotherhood.)

The consequence of these ill-conceived political activities gave to Israel the opportunity to attack the Palestinian and Syrian armed forces separately. The question now arises: Will the Ba'th ideology and the al-Asad government survive such political adventures?

The recent wave of religious fundamentalism which has swept the Middle East following the takeover of power in Iran by the Ayatollah Khomeini has also greatly enhanced Israel's chances of establishing complete hegemony over the Middle East. That part of religious funda-mentalism which condemns modern life and implicitly modern technology and work systems and seeks the seclusion of women virtually de-stroys the chances of any state, organized along traditional lines, to defend itself against encroachments by a religio-ideological secular, militarized state like Israel. It is ironic that at a time when the invasion of Lebanon points to the need on the part of Middle Eastern peoples to abandon sectarianism in the face of a common enemy, sectarianism once again has gained the loyalty of a number of Arab young people. One need only look to the Kata'ib or Phalangist Maronite Christian followers in Lebanon or the equally outspoken Muslim Brotherhood of Egypt and Syria. The difference between the Phalangists and the Muslim brothers is of course significant. The Maronites use religion to legitimize political action as do the Israelis. The Muslim Brothers appear to turn to religious fundamentalism in the hope that God, not technology and modern women, will protect them from the demands of the modern world. In whatever form, the Middle East has surely had enough of one religious group trying to put the blame for its own failures upon the heads of another religious group. Yet these policies continue, particularly in Lebanon, Syria, Iran and Israel.

At this writing, the Palestinian armed forces are being escorted out of Beirut by an international force as Israel and Syria prepare for a showdown in the Beka'a Valley. For the ideological development and social changes behind the scenes, it gives me great pleasure to recommend to you Robert Olson's study.

Max Kortepeter
New York University
August 25, 1982

THE BA'TH IN SYRIA

THE IDEOLOGY OF THE BA'TH

The Arab Socialist Renaissance Party, better known as the Ba'th (Renaissance) Party, was and still claims to be dedicated to exactly what its name proclaims: the renaissance of the Arab nation by means of Arab socialism and secularism. Its ideology is a blend of European socialism and Arab nationalism originating with its two founders, Professors Michel Aflaq and Salah al-Din al-Bitar of Damascus University, who had become acquainted with socialism and Marxism while studying in France.[1]

The Ba'th's nationalistic doctrine can be traced directly to that of a predecessor on the Syrian political scene, the youth-oriented League of National Action, led by Zaki al-Arsuzi of Alexandretta.[2] The League, which lasted from 1932 until 1940, and its offshoot, the National Arab Party, founded by al-Arsuzi after he quit the League in 1939, advanced four basic theses: The Arabs are one nation; the Arabs have one natural leader, a political-religious leader; Arabism was the national consciousness; and the Arab was the master of his own fate. This last tenet was further amplified by a call for a return to the noble Arab virtues of the Jahiliyya, the time before the coming of Islam, because Islam, and hence the Arabs themselves, had been adulterated by the Turks and Persians.[3]

Aflaq and al-Bitar, especially Aflaq, who was the more inclined to theoretical activity, established this nationalistic foundation, welded to it the socialist doctrines with which they had become familiar in France, and thence expounded their ideology based on a theoretically inseparable trinity which became the slogan of the Ba'th-- 'Unity, Freedom and Socialism.'[4]

The ideas of unity and socialism were neither new nor exclusive and were already popular within the Arab political world. The appeal, according to Nabil Kaylani, an Arab observer, came in the 'dynamic' way Aflaq combined these with the element of national freedom, for at that time, the early and middle years of the 1940's, nearly all the Arab lands were either under direct foreign control, or at least under heavy foreign influence.   Kaylani believes it was the timeliness of the Ba'th more than its ideology or structure that gave it potential for success.[5]   If this success did not come very swiftly, it was because the language used to express Ba'thist ideology was too sophisticated for those whom Aflaq and al-Bitar were trying to reach, the peasants and workers, and because the party lacked practical politicians with the necessary 'political realism.'[6]

One focal element of the Ba'th's ideology was the idea of the inqilab, a "structural transformation. . . in the spirit and thinking of the Arab people which would revolutionize their society."[7] Aflaq gave these three essential preconditions for the success of inqilab in a 1950 essay:[8]

> First, awareness of the historical and social conditions; i.e., it (the genera-tion which will bring about the inqilab) must be aware of what the nation needs for this transformation;

> Second, moral character; i.e., they must be in the vanguard and drive out the submissive, passive tools of the (unjust) circumstances;

> Third, relief: i.e., it is not enough to understand the necessity of the trans-formation and the implicitness of their responsibility.   They must believe that destiny and history and all the circum-stances (of the Arab condition) are ready for the success of this inqilab.

With the achieving of the inqilab, the trinity of Unity, Freedom and Socialism would presumably come into being. But, as is so often the case, there was ambiguity, for Aflaq also wrote that "the trinity were indispensable ingredients for the success of the inqilab, since the ideals of unity, freedom and socialism are considered fundamental and inseparable objectives of equal importance." It shall be noted that 'equal importance' was theoretical only. In practice socialism took on a lesser importance, remaining "a wing of the nationalist movement which would develop as soon as independence was won.... The nationalists, such as the Ba'th who fought for political independence. . . subjected their Socialist ideas to a secondary role until that independence was won."[10] The assertion that medieval Islam achieved a transcendency on a collective basis is an assertation with which many scholars would disagree. A critical analysis of another of Aflaq's major works, Risala, also demands the judgement that it is speculative; its real fulfillment must come through the revolutionary inqilab.

Turning to an examination of Aflaq's trinity, one sees underlying the idea of Arab unity in Ba'thist doctrine the supposition that the Arab nation (community) is a "permanent entity in history...considered, philosophically speaking, not as a social and economic historic formation, but as a transcendant fact inspiring different forms, one of its highest contributions taking the form of Islam."[11] This assertion, too, is embedded in the beliefs and ideas of Arab history, namely, that medieval Islam achieved a transcendency on a collective basis.

A German scholar, Werner Schmucker, has pointed out inconsistencies in this aspect of Aflaq's thought. Schmucker states that Aflaq emphasizes the connection between unity and socialism, and adheres to a program in which socialism of the body designates the unity of the soul. The people play a central role in this ideology because it is only through their strengths that the principal idea of the state of the soul and the eternal life of the nation can be made fruitful. Despite Aflaq's claims, the unity of freedom and socialism remains problematic for Aflaq. On the one hand, his thought promotes a view of things which is utopian and vital, and which allows for the free functioning of individual and community. On the other hand, because of his influence by orthodox Marxism and its insistence upon the functioning of the system for the benefit of the material man and his production, he suggests that the individual is subordinate to the needs of the national revolution in times of emergency - a condition, one might add, which has obtained in Syria and, indeed, the entire Arab world in the past thirty years. The ambiguity caused by the two elements leads to an unclear position of 'Spirit' and 'Matter' (material things) in the Ba'th system as a whole.

Finally, there are many-sided distinctions between the meanings of unity and freedom. Aflaq attributes these fundamental elements to the historical development of the Arabs. He states that individual freedom and collective unity are the consistent elements of Arab history. In this scheme of history the Ba'th represent only a portion of the total community, but they also hold that a (total) community destroys itself if it allows the tyranny of the collective over the individual.

The difficulty of reconciling Aflaq's thoughts on unity, freedom and socialism are embedded in the ambiguity and imprecise nature of Aflaq's thought. When he attempts to explain his thoughts, emotional issues and mannerisms often intertwine themselves in his efforts. This confronts the individual with considerable difficulty when he attempts to understand let alone participate in inqilab. The major problem is that Aflaq presumes an indefinable, intuitive, perception 'with the head' or 'inner persuasion.' This is an irrational, religious presumption, but Aflaq insists that this internal condition is the indispensable and absolutely essential basis for the Arab struggle.

Aflaq is partially aware of the disparity, if not the irreconcilability of his abstract (Risala) and concrete (inqilab) thought. He suggests several elements which will aid in the transition from speculative to concrete action:

(1)   The obtaining of knowledge (wa'y) in the sense of conviction will aid in blending the individual person- ality with the collective will. This transition serves to create a revolutionary consciousness.

(2)   A code of responsibility or sacred obligation to pursue inqilab.

(3)   Aflaq declares a need for a 'Great Experiment,' that would act as a speeding up process to bring it about under Arab conditions. He finds its model in the national and human mission of the Arab prophets. The experiment should lead to the establishment of an economic new order and a new dedication to the national will.[12]

Aflaq realizes that attainment of the 'Great Experiment' (salvation?) must come through pain

and sacrifice. This alone would lead to resurrec-
tion. The very words Aflaq chooses are biblical
and give this portion of his writings a Christian
flavor. This could account for the charge in the
barrage of propaganda coming from Iraq after 1963
that the Syrian Ba'th party was 'too Christian.'
Since Aflaq was in Iraq at this time, apparently
this charge was made with his permission.

Not only does Aflaq's Marxism clash with his
Christianity, further ambiguity is added because
of the Rousseauistic background he gives for the
nationalistic meaning of ideology. Aflaq asserts
that Rousseau's 'General Will' has meaning on the
personal level in the sense that the individual
personality reaches the level of its highest development through consciousness of the 'National
Arab Will.' The individual will identify with the
anonymous, eternal will of the people. The individual will is subordinate to, and identifies
with, the National General Will.

In assessing Aflaq's and Ba'thist ideological
origins one should notice its deep roots in the
folk history of the Arabs: the promise of a new
order which will reconcile the paradoxical elements and produce a 'Golden Age.' This explains
in part why Aflaq's 'Great Experiment', Marxist
explanations notwithstanding, requires a certain
Christian leap of faith. One should note that the
historical importance of the Ba'th is that it
seemed or was meant to embody the 'Great Experiment' that would encompass and bring to fruition
all of the rises and falls of Arab history with
the unification of the masses as the main goal.

In the late 1960's and in the 1970's it became commonplace among scholars as well as other
individuals to detail the failure of the Ba'th
ideology as expressed in the 1940's and 1950's.
While much of the criticism is accurate, it should
be noted that many of the compromises as well as

the differences which the Ba'th in Syria and Iraq
have experienced are in part due largely to the
contradictions which the 'Ba'th Synthesis' eluci-
dated.

There also remains the essential imprint of
Aflaq's influence on the development of Ba'th
thought.   He possessed and wrote of a unique view
of Islamic-Arab history and national philosophy.
His definition of 'Spirit' and 'Material' are
inseparably linked to his hard-to-fathom personality.   These confusing terms in turn led to
misunderstandings about the implication of the
concepts he uses and, at times, they lead to
ideological vagueness.[13]

The Ba'th considered the Arab states to be
merely 'regions' of the Arab nation, which included "the entire area between the Taurus and the
Sahara and the Atlantic and the Arab (Persian)
Gulf."[14]

The struggle for unification of this vast
area was devised not only for ending political
boundaries but also as a regenerative process
leading to the reform of Arab character and society.[15]   To achieve this the Arabs had to liberate
themselves from all "regional, religious and
communal loyalties" and "submit to the eternal
values of mankind."[16]

But the first obstacle to be overcome was the
political boundaries which parcelled the Arab nation.   The current boundaries were considered to
be artificially and arbitrarily drawn by the[17]
imperialist powers and by colonialism.   Aflaq
referred to the problem of colonialism in a March,
1957, speech:[18]

Our movement sees colonialism more
as a result than as a cause, a result of
whatever defects and distortions adul-
terate our society. . .

. . . The atmosphere created by
previous movements. . . was a false atmosphere which concealed from the
people the reality of the problem.
They did not want to hear that our
problem was connected to every human
problem.   They did not accept that the
stage of our struggle against colonialism
was connected to our social struggle at
home.   They did not understand or
deem it right that our problem, in all
Arab regions, was one problem, that
the unification of the struggle was
necessary, that the separation which
had been imposed on our land was
artificial and obstructive, and that in
the hearts of the people was a guaran-
tee that the rust would be cleared, that
the falseness (of the separation) would
disappear and that the fact that our
nation was one nation would become
apparent.

Just as socialism was tied to unity and
anticolonialism, so too was it tied to freedom,
which Aflaq wrote should be "conceived not merely
as emancipation from political tyranny and oppres-
sive poverty, but the liberation of the Arab people, unified in mind and spirit, joined together
in social brotherhood.   Freedom should, therefore,
emanate from the very soul of the Arab and be
cherished as an indivisable part of his heri-
tage."[19]
    Thus, in the early and middle 1940's, nearly
a decade before the rise of Gamal Abd al-Nasir in
Egypt, the Ba'th leaders became the most consistent and inflexible anticolonialists and 'neutral-
ists' of the Arab world.[20]
    The Arab socialism formulated by the Ba'th in

the opinion of one author, was partly to counter
the appeal of communism and had as its objective[21]
the freeing of man's talents and abilities.
This implied a destruction of the influence of the
traditional aristocracy of wealth which had ruled
the Arab countries for generations, so that lower
classes would be able to break out of the economic
grip which held them in a depressed state and
which blocked their political influence.[22]

In original Ba'thist dialectics there was
little preoccupation with the Marxist concept of
the class struggle. Aflaq recognized the class
struggle as a "law of historical evolution," but
wrote that "Marxism. . . greatly deviated from it
and exaggerated it" by putting it in an international context and by ignoring the vital historical formation of nationalism when the links joining the working and exploited class in all countries of the world were weaker by far than the
links joining a specific class in a specific country to its nationalism."[23]

Aflaq took great pains to point out the differences between Ba'thism and communism, as in a
1950 essay in which he listed what he considered
to be the four major theoretical differences between the two:[24]

>   (1) The meaning of socialism in
> the communist system is not limited to
> economic organization, but obeys ends
> and aims derived from the communist
> system. . .
>   As for Ba'ath socialism, its mean-
> ing is limited to the economic organiza-
> tion which aims at restoring supervision
> in distributing the wealth of the Arab
> nation, at establishing bases for the
> economy so as to guarantee economic
> equality and justice among the citi-

zens...

(2) Communist socialism is imprinted with communist philosophy, which comes as a product of a specific society. . . Our socialism is imprinted with our philosophy originating from the needs of Arab society, its historical conditions and its special circumstances.

(3) Communist philosophy rests on belief in materialism and explains the evolution of history and societies by the economic element alone. . . (Our) philosophy does not agree with this materialistic view; instead, it considers the intellectual and spiritual element of great influence in the evolution of history and the development of mankind. . .

(4) Communist philosophy does not attach great importance to the individdual and does not respect him. . . Our socialism depends on the individual and liberates his individuality; it does not condone the destruction of personal freedom. It respects all individuals as equals and has no room for the existence of an absolute dictatorship.

In the same essay Aflaq also sets forth the practical differences between Ba'thism and communism. He claimed that communist socialism had led to too much nationalization, loss of property rights, loss of individual initiative, and loss of inheritance rights. These were things which the Ba'th did not sanction and would not do, although in the case of inheritance, the party had placed limitations on it, leaving it almost theoretical in some situations and merely an abstract right in others.[25]

Aflaq claimed also that "communist socialism is limited because it is based on an economic phi-losophy--Marxism--which holds economic and histo-rical views that today are unable to withstand genuine scientific criticism."[26]

In this same essay Aflaq emphasized the dif-ferences between Ba'th socialism and the National Socialism of Nazism, writing that National Social-ism was based on "the superiority of one kind (of people) over another and their right to dominate the world," as well as on "differences between nationals of the same nation, which leads to the dictatorship of an individual or class."[27]

A more pressing problem for Aflaq was recon-ciling Ba'thist socialism with Islam. He tried to do this in part by a reversal: instead of having Ba'thism conform to Islam, Islam must conform to 'Arabism,'[28] which in Ba'thist ideology meant 'the feeling and consciousness of being Arab."[29]

Aflaq's major attempt at effecting this re-conciliation came in a 1956 essay:[30]

> Do youth consider that Islam was a
> revolutionary movement at the time of
> its appearance, rebelling against things
> which were established: beliefs, cus-
> toms and interest?   And then do they
> consider that only revolutionaries can
> truly understand Islam?   This is natur-
> al, because the revolutionary situation
> is   an   eternal,   inseparable   and
> unchangeable situation; it has the same
> psychological conditions and also, to a
> large   extent,   the   same   objective
> conditions.   It is very strange--and
> this you should think about and
> consider--that the visible defenders of

Islam who demonstrate more zeal than others. . . are the farthest elements from revolution at our present stage. Therefore it is inconceivable that they understand Islam.   Consequently, it is very natural that the people closest to Islam in understanding, sentiment and harmony are the revolutionary genera-tion, the generation rebelling against the corrupt old.

The conscious Arab was one who realized the dynamic and revolutionary nature of Islam.   This consciousness for Aflaq became 'Arabism.'

Such theorizing was fine, but in practice the relationship between the Ba'th and Islamic ele-ments in Syrian society was somewhat different.[31] The Ba'th did not challenge Islamic institutions such as Ramadan, the month of fasting, although a less secular-at least in ideology-Tunisia, dis-couraged observance of the fast because of its counter-productive aspects.

Another problem Aflaq faced in formulating his ideology was the question of what to do with minorities.   Syria, besides Sunni (or Orthodox) Muslims, has significant numbers of Arabs belong-ing to various Christian churches and heterodox Muslim sects, especially Isma'ilis, Alawis and Druzes.   There is also a substantial number of Sunni Kurds, a non-Arab people indigenous to parts of Syria, Iraq, Iran and Turkey.   The Arab sectar-ian minorities presented little problem since they were Arabs; indeed, Aflaq himself was a member of the Greek Orthodox Church, al-Bitar was a Sunni, and many of the leaders of the Ba'th especially since the early 1960's, have been Alawis.   But the Kurds, who are non-Arabs, and had been in almost continual revolt against the Arab state of Iraq, presented quite another problem.

Theoretically, the 'renaissance' from which
the party took its name was to end all factional
distinctions, whether religious, communal, tribal,
racial or regional. But Aflaq himself belied this
theory when he would not allow Kurdish members of
Akram Hawrani's Arab Socialist Party to join the
Ba'th when the two parties merged in 1953.[32]

This contradiction between theory and practice came to be a rather regular occurrence. This
dilemma is even more evident after the Ba'th came
to power in Syria. Not only did the Ba'th in
Syria actively help Iraq (at least when they were
on speaking terms with the Iraqis), fight its
Kurdish rebels, but they also clamped down on the
Kurds in Syria. Many Kurds were expelled across
the border into Turkey, which had 'solved' its
Kurdish problem by simply claiming that the Kurds
were "mountain Turks" who had forgotten their
native language.[33]   Thousands were stripped of
their citizenship, and many others were simply
declared to be foreigners even though they had
valid Syrian identification cards. The Ba'th also
refused to apply land reform measures in areas
where Kurds would have received land. After 1967,
when the Neo-Ba'th were firmly in power, pressure
on the Kurds in Syria was eased, ironically, to
increase pressure on Iraq with whom relations were
becoming increasingly bitter.[34]

By that time Aflaq had become persona non
grata to the Syrian Ba'th, although he was a kind
of 'godfather' to the Iraqi branch of the Ba'th,
which was to seize power again in Baghdad in
1968.[35]   While in Baghdad, Aflaq gave a speech on
10 June 1969 in which he again addressed himself
to the question of the Kurds, who were in
rebellion in northern Iraq:[36]

The party does not object to the
Kurds' right to have their own govern-

ment, but. . . the Kurdish insurrection
in Iraq is an object of exploitation by
imperialistic and reactionary forces--
even though the Kurdish movement does
rely on national feelings among the
Kurds, feelings which are legitimate and
unsuspicious, but the imperialistic and
reactionary powers exploit them and
distort their goals...

The majority of the Kurds are
found in two non-Arab countries, while
the part found in Iraq is a relatively
small minority. Secondly, the situation
of the Kurds in the Arab Nation differs
entirely from their situation in the two
countries where they are in great numbers: Turkey and Iran. For long centuries the Kurds have lived with the
Arabs and until now no distinction between them. . . has been known. . .
Consequently, any suppression, or op-
pression, was as though on one people,
while during this shared history their
political and military heroes were also
heroes of the Arabs. (This) shows
very clearly that the Kurdish movement
in the Arab Nation, and especially in
Iraq, is the object of imperialistic
exploitation because the Arab Nation is
the least suitable nation for the
appearance of a (Kurdish) rebellion.

This excerpt, besides illuminating Aflaq's
views on the Kurdish question, serves to point out
another facet of the Ba'thist dialectics of the
1960's--the 'Marxification' of the party's terminology.

Although Marxist terminology had been present
in the party's writings since its beginnings, the

meanings had often been rearranged to suit Aflaq's own needs. In addition, the small Marxist wing of the party, present since the first pan-Arab congress in 1947, had wielded only minimal influence in the 1940's and 1950's.[37]

But the 1961 breakup of the United Arab Republic, coupled with the failure of the two Ba'thist governments which came to power in Baghdad and Damascus in the spring of 1963 to form a federal union, had thoroughly undermined the traditional assumptions of Ba'thist ideology. This development was felt even more keenly in view of the ideological developments in the other revolutionary regimes of the Arab world, which tended to emphasize the social commitments of the national revolution, and of the developments in the communist world which tended to emphasize the national character of the tasks along the road to socialism.[38]

Such confusion gave the small group of earlier Marxists the opportunity to have an influential hand in developing a new ideology for the party: an ideology which came to be espoused by radical opponents of Aflaq and al-Bitar called the neo-Ba'th.[39]

The most prominent architect of this new ideology was a former communist, Yassin al-Hafiz, who published in February 1963, a month before the coup which brought the Ba'th to power in Syria, an article criticizing Ba'thist ideology from a Marxist point of view and offering his own proposals for its ideological rejuvenation.[40]

Al-Hafiz berated the Ba'th for ambiguity in its trinity, especially concerning liberty which he wrote could only be achieved by means of a popular democracy restricting the freedom of reactionary groups, giving complete freedom to workers, and keeping the army out of politics.[41]

The military officers within the Ba'th were

how do dems wr-le x a d ?

quick to accept al-Hafiz's concept of liberty. It
coincided with their desire to limit a parliamentary form of government by the bourgeoisie, in
their minds, a reactionary force.   In this respect
al-Hafiz rejected the traditional doctrine of the
party and of its founder, Aflaq. This aspect of
his doctrine now enabled the Ba'th to give a progressive hue to its policies. At the same time
the military group within the Ba'th rejected al-
Hafiz's argument that the army should not be allowed to interfere in strictly political affairs.[42]

When the Sixth National Congress met in
Damascus in October 1963, the Marxists managed to
introduce before the Congress draft resolutions
patterned almost wholesale after Hafiz's article.
These resolutions, although stripped of almost all
of their original intent, formed the basis of a
document adopted by the Congress, called A Few
Theoretical Propositions. The Propositions, although signalling in many ways the advent of the
new ideology on a legitimized basis, adopted the
terminology of the Marxists while twisting or
completely changing the meanings.[43]

The Congress accepted a phrase put forth by
the Marxists, 'the Arab way to socialism,' as a
starting point for formulating the new socialist
doctrine. But it rejected the adjunct proposal to
do away with the term 'Arab socialism.' The Marxists claimed that this was incorrect because all
socialism was the same, no matter what country
practiced it, and only the way to socialism differed from country to country.[44]

Also included was Hafiz's reworking of the
Ba'thist concept of liberty. The section setting
forth the notion that liberty requires popular
democracy followed Hafiz's article almost verba-
tim.[45] However, the Propositions, as finally
approved by the Congress, rejected al-Hafiz's

admonition to keep the army out of politics on the
grounds that only through military involvement
could popular democracy be achieved. This paved
the way for a more politicized military and more
intervention in the affairs of the party and in
Syrian politics.[46] The government accepted the
Congress's version.

Ba'thist dialectics also began to include the
Marxist notion of 'popular struggle' within Syria
to marshal support for the regime and to ensure
its hegemony. The Neo-Ba'thists came to regard
'popular struggle' as the only means to combat the
arch-enemy: Israel. This concept of popular
struggle or, as it was called when referring to
Israel, 'people's war of liberation,' was largely
derived from the Algerian war of independence in
which several of the radicals had served as volun-
teers.[47] Ben-Tzur described what popular struggle
meant to the party with regard to Syria. The
'popular struggle' became an inclusive slogan to
be used against opponents of the regime. At the
end of 1966 it was used by the government in a
dispute with the Iraq Petroleum Company. Subsequently it began to be used more extensively, even
by Muftis in their Friday sermons against enemies
identified by the regime.[48]

By this time the radicals of the Neo-Ba'th
were firmly in control of Syria and had ousted the
old guard, officially expelling Aflaq from the
party (an action which had little effect outside
Syria). For the Syrian Ba'th, the metamorphosis
from a moderate socialist to a more radical Marxist party, which exemplified the Neo-Ba'th in its
heyday, was complete.

Chapter II

ORIGINS AND EARLY YEARS OF THE BA'TH

In the first chapter it was noted that the Arab Socialist Renaissance Party was founded in Damascus in the early 1940's by two professors at Damascus University, Michel Aflaq and Salah al-Din al-Bitar. Both men were born in Damascus shortly before the start of World War I--sources give various dates between 1910 and 1912. Aflaq was a Greek Orthodox, al-Bitar, a Sunni Muslim. Both were educated at the Sorbonne, Aflaq in history and al-Bitar in physics and mathematics. After completing their studies, they returned to Damascus in 1934 to teach.

Some of their earliest political contacts during their students days were with the French Communist Party for whose paper Aflaq occasionally wrote articles. As far as can be ascertained, neither actually joined the party, although they maintained contact with it after their return to Syria. The two men broke nearly all ties with the communists in 1936 when, according to Aflaq, they decided that communism, with its emphasis on internationalism, would not be viable in the Arab world.

This break was followed by several years of relative inaction politically. Aflaq later explained this inaction by writing that the break with the communists:

> ...caused in us a spiritual and intellectual crisis which interrupted our writing and political activity for about two years. This was the case because we were not politicians who don a different garment to suit each occasion and disguise their mistakes with

specious argument.   We wanted above all to explain things to ourselves; and to explain to ourselves and to the nation something more profound than politics--namely the Arab mind and soul.[2]

By 1940 the ideas of Aflaq and al-Bitar were beginning to take shape. They gathered a small group of adherents and, as often happens in the Arab world, they set up a party which they called the Ba'th. They issued their first broadsheet early in 1941, directing it against both the French and the National Bloc government then in power which represented traditional interests in Syria. In that same year they organized support for Rashid Ali al-Ghaylani's revolt in Iraq against the British.[3] For this they were sent to prison where they met Akram Hawrani who had actually gone into Iraq to help the rebels against the British. Hawrani later formed the Arab Socialist Party (ASP).[4]

Aflaq and al-Bitar left teaching in 1942 to devote all their time and energies to political activity--mobilizing students, publishing clandestine broadsheets and organizing suq (market) strikes. Aflaq ran for parliament in 1943 and was defeated. Al-Bitar was sent to a detention camp in Palmyra for part of 1944 and 1945 in a French effort to cool him off politically. After he returned and rejoined Aflaq, the erstwhile politicians founded a party newspaper, appropriately called al-Ba'th in 1946. They convened the party's first national (pan-Arab) congress in 1947. At this congress they drew up the party's constitution. Most of the delegates were Sunnis and Orthodox Christians from the urban petite bourgeoisie or members of the country gentry.[5]

Aflaq ran for parliament again in the elections of July, 1947, in which the Ba'th joined with Hawrani's ASP, the communists and other progressives to force the government of President Shukri al-Quwwatli to change the election laws to allow universal male suffrage and one-stage direct elections.   Despite the changes, along with the Ba'th and the ASP, Aflaq was defeated in an election obviously rigged through military intimidation of voters opposed to the government.[6]

However, Quwwatli's government was forced to resign on 29 November 1948, under the pressure of popular resentment following the debacle of the first Arab-Israeli war.   Khalid al-Azm, a Western-educated Damascus businessman and politician, formed a new government two weeks later; it remained in power until 29 March 1949 when Colonel Husni al-Za'im, with hints of help from the American embassy and military advisors, seized power in what was to become the first of a series of rapid-fire coups.[7]

Al-Za'im in turn lasted only until 14 August, when another colonel, Sami Hinnawi, ousted him and had him executed.   Hinnawi too had outside help, notably from Iraq, and probably from the British.[8]

The Ba'th had supported al-Za'im, who extended the voting franchise to literate women, set up a modern civil code, abolished family-controlled waqfs (charitable, usually religious, foundations often set up not only as charity but as tax dodges and entrusted to the supervision of family members), and proposed both a new constitution ending sectarian representation and a system of land re-distribution.[9]   Despite their support for al-Za'im, the Ba'th fared even better under Hinnawi.   Aflaq became minister of education and his friend Hawrani, minister of agriculture.   These new posts did not prevent

Aflaq from being defeated for the third time in a
bid for a seat in parliament.   He left the
government charging fraud.[10]

Under Hinnawi, traditionalists in the People's Party, an anti-Quwwatli offshoot of the
National Bloc led by northern Syrians (particularly the powerful al-Tasi family of Homs), began
pressing for a union with Iraq.   The Ba'th was
inclined to support this move, but Hawrani,
deeply suspicious of any union involving the
Hashimite family then ruling Iraq, persuaded
Aflaq to oppose the suggestion.   At the same time
Hawrani tried to induce Colonel Adib al-Shishakli,
who had served with Hawrani in the 1948 war in
Palestine, to stage a coup.   On 19 December
1949, with a Syrian- Iraqi union imminent,
al-Shishakli overthrew Hinnawi.

Following the coup al-Shishakli maintained a
low profile in Syrian politics, although he clearly remained the most powerful person in the
country.   His desire for power then became
stronger, and he staged a second coup, this one
on 19 November 1951, through which he set up a
personal regime.   All political parties were
outlawed, including Shishakli's two staunchest
supporters-- the Ba'th and the ASP.   In their
place Shishakli established another party
controlled by himself, which he dubbed the Arab
Liberation Movement (ALM)

Both the Ba'th and the ASP worked to
depose Shishakli; Hawrani apparently went so far
as to set in motion plans for another coup.   But
in December 1952, al-Shishakli struck first,
ordering the arrest of all Ba'th, ASP and
communist leaders.   Hawrani, Aflaq and al-Bitar
departed for Lebanon--there is some evidence that
they were permitted to leave instead of escaping--
where they further cemented the ties that would
lead to the merger of their two parties in 1953.[11]

In July 1953, when al-Shishakli held carefully controlled elections in which his ALM won 72 of 82 seats, a group of opposition leaders secretly met in Homs to sign a "National Pact" vowing to overthrow al-Shishakli. Apparently unaware of what was happening, al-Shishakli declared a general amnesty, allowing all the exiles to return to Syria. Hawrani immediately took advantage of the amnesty to strengthen his ties with the military and to plan for another attempt to oust his former comrade.[12]

A Druze uprising was to be the signal, but the arrest of the Druze notable and Ba'th member, Mansur al-Atrash, set off a premature riot. Al-Shishakli declared martial law, but with the occurrence of a widespread army mutiny--only the Damascus garrison refused to participate--he saw the light, resigned and, on 25 February 1954, left Syria for Europe.[13]

As mentioned above, the ASP and the Ba'th had merged in 1953. The ASP soon constituted the left wing of the party, now officially called the Arab Ba'th Socialist Party. The Ba'th's bitter experiences over the preceding five years--with al-Za'im, Hinnawi and al-Shishakli--made them wary of letting military leaders meddle in politics. Consequently, they tried to use Hawrani's close contacts with officers as a means of dissuading the military from acting too forcefully after al-Shishakli's resignation and were able to pave the way for a return to civilian government.[14]

Parliamentary elections were scheduled for September 1954. The Addition of the ASP had given the Ba'th the vitally important numerical support it had previously lacked; the party now boasted a hard-core nucleus of some 6,000 members, large by Syrian standards. As a result, the Ba'th candidates were especially

strong in the areas of Damascus, Hama, Homs and
the Jebel al-Druze whence they derived much of
their support. Added to this newly-found
strength was the disintegration of the
conservative parties which entered separate
candidates who attacked each other more often
than they did their liberal opponents.[15]
   At this time the Ba'th was the only party,
with the exception of the communists, that had a
detailed program which addressed the issues and
problems facing Syria. It opposed all foreign,
not only Western, influence in Syria. It was
anti-Iraqi, anti-Hashimite and anti-Soviet. One of
the historians who recorded these events has
stated that throughout the campaign the Ba'th
refused to cooperate with the communist party
despite the repeated appeal of Khalid al-Baqdash,
the Syrian communist leader, for a 'National
Front.'[16]
   Conducted by the less-political caretaker
government which took over after al-Shishakli's
resignation, and using secret ballots and enclosed
voting booths, this election has been called, with
some justification, "the first free election in the
Arab world."[17] Of 142 seats, 64 went to independents, 30 to the People's Party and 22 to the
Ba'th. These results showed four outstanding
features: the strength of the Ba'th (in 1949 it
had won only one of 214 seats); the decline by
half of the number of seats going to the People's
Party;the mass of independents who would become
the object of party politicking to get their
support on every vital matter; and, finally, the
election of Khalid al-Baqdash, the first communist
elected to parliament in any Arab state.[18]
   Of the leading Ba'thists, Hawrani and four
others were elected in Hama and al-Bitar in
Damascus. Aflaq did not run, claiming that it
was not his style and that he preferred discourse

with a small circle of disciples.[19]   But it is also
possible that he had become tired of running and
losing.

When parliament met, Nizam al-Qudsi of the
People's Party was chosen President of the Cham-
ber.   He asked Faris al-Khuri, a distinguished
Protestant jurist and statesman, to form a
government. Al-Khuri, then 77 years old, was a
political independent and a well-known veteran of
both the anti-Ottoman and anti-French struggles.
His government was dominated by the People's
Party, with the National Party in a secondary
position, mainly because the Ba'th and other
leftist parties refused to participate in a coalition
government.   His government did not last long; it
fell victim to the heated debates over the
Baghdad Pact, the Western-inspired counterpart
of NATO and SEATO, and the Cairo-Baghdad
Arab Collective Security Pact (ACSP). Opponents
of the government, led by the Ba'th, used
al-Khuri's ill-timed remark that Iraq would not
have had to join the Baghdad Pact if the ACSP
had been effective enough to bring down the
government.[20]

Sabri al-Asali, a leader of the anti-Iraqi
faction in the National Party, then became
premier.   The two strongmen of the new government however were Khalid al-Azm and Sami
Hawrani, the latter of whom acted behind the
scenes.[21]

Following the change in government, the
Egyptians and Saudis, then on reasonably good
terms, pressed Syria to subscribe to their alternative to the Baghdad Pact. This was a treaty
which would create economic, military and political cooperation among Arab states opposed to the
Baghdad Pact. Syria, caught between both
camps, hesitated. The pressure from both sides
mounted. This was coupled with increased Israeli

aggressiveness along the border. Nasir's arms deal with Czechoslovakia helped push Syria into closer relations with the Soviet Union, from whom, it was thought, aid could be received with no visible strings attached.[22]

After the Soviet-Syrian rapprochement, the Ba'th began cooperating once again with the Syrian Communist Party. Although they still reiterated constantly the ideological differences between the two parties, they often used what came to be a slogan: "We may meet in the same trenches, but we can't join up with them."[23]

At this point in Syrian affairs a political assassination drew the Ba'th and communists even closer together and caused violent reaction and misunderstanding abroad. The victim was a popular young deputy chief-of-staff, Lieutenant Colonel Adnan al-Malki, the brother of a leading Ba'thist. He was the officer on whom the Ba'th counted to keep the military in check and maintain enough pro-Ba'thist sentiment among the officer corps to prevent another party from being able to use the army against the Ba'th. The assassin was a military policeman and a member of the conservative Syrian Social Nationalist Party (SSNP).

The consequences of the killing were the arrest of 130 SSNP members on charges relating to the murder and the elimination of the SSNP from the Syrian political scene. This move provided a chance for the communists to educate the Ba'th by charging foreign, especially American, instigation of the murder and the flight en masse of SSNP members to Beirut where they portrayed the affair as an indication of a communist threat on Syria. The latter charge stimulated Western fears which led to counter-measures. Western efforts to block communist influence led in turn to a real opportunity for Soviet involvement in Syria.[24]

An almost immediate result of the closer Syrian-Soviet ties engendered by the aftermath of the al-Malki assassination was the signing of arms agreements with the USSR, Czechoslovakia and East Germany. Concomitant with the growing Egyptian-Soviet and Syrian-Soviet ties was a burgeoning sentiment for Syria to enter some kind of union with Egypt. Added impetus for union came in June 1956, when the government of Sa'id al-Chazzi, formed the previous September, fell. It was to be replaced by one headed by al-Asali. The new government was supported by a hodge-podge of mutually hostile groups, including the Ba'th, which made its support contingent on the beginning of unity talks with Cairo, a condition to which al-Asali readily agreed.[25]

These negotiations never really got underway before Iraq, alarmed by the growing closeness of Egypt and Syria and the Ba'th and the communists, began plotting to get rid of the two Syrian parties, thus setting back Cairo-Damascus relations. The plan, which soon included many right-wing Syrians, was uncovered during the 1956 Arab-Israeli war.[26]

The Iraqis need not have been so upset because the Ba'th-communist honeymoon was soon over. The Ba'th, suspicious of the communists because of their foreign ties and unhappy with the obvious American concern over the growth of communist influence in Syria, stopped cooperating with the Syrian communists during the summer of 1957.[27]

Unfortunately, Iraq and Turkey were also very much concerned over the almost total takeover of Syria by leftist parties, not simply the communists. Both nations massed troops on their borders with Syria. Hawrani, elected speaker in the parliament, postponed the elections

scheduled for November 1957, while al-Bitar met
with the U.S. ambassador to the United Nations,
Henry Cabot Lodge, in New York. In the
meantime, Norman Thomas, head of the American
Socialist Party, went to Damascus to declare
American popular support for non-communist
socialism. Khalid al-Azm, already minister of
defense, became deputy premier in December
1957. The Ba'th described this last event as
foreshadowing a communist takeover and, with
military support, stampeded Syria into the "total"
union Nasser had demanded. Hawrani and others
had differed from the Ba'th in that they wanted a
federal union, but their concern over the events
outlined above made them so eager for union that
they agreed to Nasir's demands.[28]

Chapter III

UNION AND SECESSION

The Ba'th had maneuvered Syria into union after the first talks had bogged down by encouraging the army to conduct its own negotiations with Egypt. The army agreed, and, on 12 January 1958 a 14-member delegation of officers went to Cairo, asking Nasir for an immediate union of the two armies as a prelude to the union of the two nations. This move was taken without consulting the government in Damascus to which the officers sent an ultimatum demanding union. Damascus sent al-Bitar--who had urged the officers to go to Cairo in the first place--to meet with the delegation. Instead, without any authorization to do so, al-Bitar met with Nasir to negotiate a political union.

In this meeting Nasir insisted on an unconditional and complete union with the abolition of all political parties. Al-Bitar and the Ba'th hastily accepted and the Syrian government had little choice but to go along with the already-announced union. Quwwatli, again premier, and Nasir formally proclaimed the establishment of the United Arab Republic on the first of February. Both parliaments ratified the union four days later and on 21 February 1958 referendums in both nations confirmed the action and elected Nasir president by 99.9 percent majorities.

One obvious question arising out of the impromptu union negotiations was why the Ba'th had accepted Nasir's stipulation that political parties be disbanded and replaced by his National Union Party. Malcolm Kerr wrote in The Arab Cold War that the Ba'th sought union in a spirit of desperation and fear of their own inability to maintain control in Syria. They seemed to have imagined that once the union was formed they would not only see their rivals eliminated through the weight of 'Abd al--Nasir's prestige, but that they would also hold their own against him.[2]

Aflaq and the other Ba'th leaders were not too dismayed at having to dissolve the party because they believed that Nasir would give them the task of setting up the Syrian branch of the National Union Party which they would naturally dominate and because they would play the major political and ideological role in Syria and elsewhere in the Arab World. Then, too, they decided to maintain a discreet identity and organization even if officially disbanded.[3]

Nasir, it turned out, was not willing to share power and prestige with anyone. Instead, he made conciliatory gestures by appointing Hawrani and al-Asali vice-presidents and al-Bitar a minister of state in the Cairo-based central government; al-Bitar later became minister of culture and national guidance. Within Syria Hawrani was made president of the Syrian Executive Council while Ba'thists held the ministries of economy, agriculture and labor and social affairs. A Ba'th sympathizer, Abd al-Hamid al-Sarraj, held the relatively powerful post of minister of the interior giving him control over the Syrian security network. Nasir kept all the real power and all decisions were made by him in Cairo.[4]

Nasir tightened control in Syria following the 14 July 1958 coup in Iraq in which Abd al-Karim Qasim overthrew the Hashimite ruling family. He placed the Syrian Executive Council directly under the control of the central UAR government, hence under his personal control, relieving Hawrani as its head and bringing him to Cairo as central minister of justice.[5]

Meanwhile the rift between Nasir and the Ba'th steadily widened. The Ba'thists in Syria and Iraq instigated a revolt aimed at ousting Qasim and bringing Iraq into the UAR; it was easily quashed. Angered by this rash action, by the Ba'th's intimations that they had provided him with a philosophy and an ideology, and by the Ba'th's obstructing the formation of the Syrian branch of his National Union Party, Nasir decided to deal with the Ba'th and set up his party with one blow. He scheduled elections to the National Union Assembly for 8 July 1959. Aware of the fact that the Ba'th leaders were blamed by many Syrians for the Egyptian exploitation of the Syrian economy caused by the merger, Nasir allowed the Syrian elections to be largely free from governmental interference, so that the Ba'th would be humiliated by the Syrians themselves. Nasir's adviser for Syrian affairs, Mahmud al-Riad, met with prominent conservatives to draw up an anti-Ba'th campaign, even including public demonstrations. The Ba'th, taken aback, withdrew many of its candidates and won only 250 out of 9,445 seats. The irony of the situation is that Nasir, so ardently supported by the Ba'th, had turned to their arch-rivals, the reactionaries, to humiliate the Ba'th--by means of a free election![6]

The Ba'th was in disarray and began to fragment. At the Fourth National Congress in Beirut in August 1959, the delegates all but condemned the 1958 decision to dissolve the Syrian branch of the party. Some members of that branch were trying to rebuild it within Syria; another group had quit, working independently; and a third, an extreme pro-Nasirist group, was expelled and later set up a rival party, also called the Ba'th, to support the union. To make matters worse, Aflaq and al-Bitar were squabbling with Hawrani, who wanted to begin an active opposition to Nasir and

the UAR.   Aflaq and al-Bitar, however, because
the Ba'th could not operate legally as a party in
Syria or, in view of its past record, openly oppose the union, felt they should begin a "passive
resistance"--actual but unadmitted.   They did so;
Hawrani began boycotting all government functions.[7]

Nasir-Ba'th relations deteriorated further.
Feeling betrayed by Nasir's actions in the election and by his rapproachment with Jordan, Saudi
Arabia and the United States to counteract
Qasim's growing influence in the Arab world, the
Ba'th ministers resigned en masse from the
government in December 1959 making it Nasir's
turn to feel betrayed.   In spite of what he had
done to the Ba'th in the election, Nasir still felt
that he deserved more support from people who
had practically come begging him for union.
Unwilling to give up Egyptian dominance, yet at
the same time unable to pick up other Syrian
allies, Nasir came to depend on personal control,
exercised through his closest associates in Syria,
Field Marshall Abd al-Hakim Amir and Colonel
al-Sarraj, who had cast his lot with the Egyptians.   This amounted to tacit admission that
Syria could only be controlled by the police and
the military.[8]

One of the more portentous Egyptian actions
was the stage-by-stage purge of the Syrian army.
Communists, progressive Hawrani supporters,
Aflaq and al-Bitar supporters and, finally,
anyone opposed to Egyptianization were systemati-
cally eliminated.   The favorite "burying ground"
for Ba'thist officers was Egypt itself; an often-
used alternative was sending them around the
world to embassy and consular posts.   Several
Ba'th officers in Egypt set up a secret military
committee there in 1959, awaiting a propitious
moment to "rectify the situation."   Led by three

Alawis, members of the closely-knit heterodox
Muslim sect from the region of Latakia (Salah
al-Jadid, Hafiz al-Asad and Muhammad Umran),
and a Druze (Hamad Ubayd) the 'Military
Committee' did not tell the civilian Ba'th leadership anything about its organization or even of
its existence.[9]

The propitious moment for ousting Egypt
came on 28 September 1961 but the officers who
took advantage of it were not the members of the
'Military Committee;' instead, they were right-
wing Syrian officers. Nasir's repression of the
left in Syria had strengthened the right and
rendered the progressives unable to act.
Hawrani and his faction of the Ba'th supported
the action of the conservative officers, the
purpose of whose coup was to enable Syria to
withdraw from the UAR a move soon made. Both
al-Bitar and Hourani signed a proclamation
backing the secession.[10]

The creation of the UAR, it seems, expressed a desire of Syria to avoid the embrace of
the great powers, especially that of the Soviet
Union, and a genuine belief in Arab unity. The
great difference between this genuinely-held
belief and its materialization forced the Syrians to
realize that they had to find their own way to
modernization. They would have to define their
own strategies of development. In an ironic
sense, the failure of the union and Egyptian
actions in Syria helped to create a greater sense
of Syrian identification which aided the
consolidation of the Ba'th during the next two
years.[11] The older ranking Ba'th members were
somewhat discredited by the whole affair allowing
second echelon members to come to the fore and
into power in 1963.[12]

The aftermath of the secession in terms of
the Ba'th party itself was the further fragmen-

tation of the party.   The Ba'th National (pan-
Arab) Command attacked the withdrawal, forcing
al-Bitar into the embarrassing position of having
to repudiate his signature on the proclamation
supporting secession, while the 'Military Committee' and most other Ba'th officers supported it.
It should be kept in mind that these officers later
changed their position on the matter when the
leader of the coup, Lieutenant Colonel Abd
al-Karim Nahlawi, cashiered them in an attempt to
rid the military of officer-politicians.   Another
group, opposed to the secession and to the tacit
Ba'th approval of it, withdrew from the party to
form the Socialist Unionist Movement (SUM) under
the leadership of Sami Sufan.[13]

After a conservative government was set up,
it called for elections in December 1961.   They
were held under many restrictions one of which
banned political parties; the conservatives easily
won, but the results concerning Ba'th candidates,
easily identifiable although not allowed to run
under the party's aegis, were illuminating.   Al-
Bitar and the candidates identified with his wing
were defeated; Hawrani and his wing, along with
some non-Ba'th allies, won 15 seats.   Working
with the veteran Khalid al-Azm, Hawrani led an
assembly campaign to rescind all political
restrictions and censorship.   Instead, the
assembly repealed most nationalization decrees,
amended the land reform law in favor of the
traditional landlords and took two minutes' time to
vote themselves a 333 percent pay raise.[14]

But Syrian political matters after the break
away from Egypt, proceeded unevenly.   In one
week in March-April 1962 army officers staged
three separate coups--one each in Damascus,
Homs and Aleppo.   The first, in Damascus on 20
March, was attempted by rightists led by
al-Nahlawi.   Three days later in Homs an odd

congregation of Ba'thists, Nasirists and independents, all acting together but for different objectives, staged a second coup. Both the Ba'thists and Nasirists wanted to get back into the military from which they had been purged by al-Nahlawi, but the Ba'th wanted to return in order to prevent al-Nahlawi from rejoining the UAR, which he threatened to do, while the Nasirists wanted to re-enter the UAR--but under their auspices, not al-Nahlawi's.

The following day, 1 April, Gen. Abd al-Karim Zahr al-Din, the commander-in-chief of the army, called a conference in Homs to patch up the cracks and restore order and unity. While he was doing that, Nasirists in Aleppo occupied the radio station there asking Egypt, unsuccessfully, to send in paratroopers and restore the union by force.[15]

Back in Homs the 41 officers meeting there reached several important decisions: al-Nahlawi and his associates, who were nearly all Damascenes, would be exiled; civilian government would be restored; the union of all Arab states was to be called for, although a proposal to rejoin the UAR was defeated. No action would be taken towards reinstating officers purged after the September coup.

These decisions, especially the latter two, angered a few officers, in particular unionists and those dismissed after al-Nahlawi's first coup, and they staged abortive coups in Homs, Aleppo and Dayr az-Zur on 2 April. The bulk of the army accepted the Hom's decisions and the coups were quickly quashed. The recent attempts at taking over the government made the military realize that it could not control Syria effectively. As a result, several leading officers agreed to set up a civilian government under Dr. Bashir al-Azma.[16]

Throughout this period of various moves and countermoves the Ba'th found itself in a dilemma: if it still wanted to be an Arab unionist party, it could not condone the secession by working within the secessionist regime. But at the same time, returning to union under Nasir was anathema to the leaders of the party. This quandary was exacerbated by antagonisms from both extremes of the party. On one hand were those who gave unqualified support to Nasir, a group led by Fuad al-Rikabi and Abdullah al-Rimawi; on the other were the supporters of Hawrani who vehemently opposed Nasir and worked with the new regime. In an effort to solve this dilemma Aflaq and the National Command, now stationed in Beirut, came up with a policy which criticized both the mistakes made during the UAR period and the secession, proposing a return to a federal union, a type of union totally unacceptable to Nasir.

Unfortunately for the Ba'thist leaders, this proposal created more internal dissension because it was also totally unacceptable to many of the younger Ba'th members, who were opposed both to union and to the continuing domination of the party by Aflaq.[17]

Aflaq arrived at a possible solution to this threat by convening the Fifth National Congress in Homs in May 1962 to which he invited a few dependable Syrians and large numbers of Iraqi Ba'thists, who supported Aflaq at that time, thereby negating the influence of his opponents. The presence of a number of Iraqis was portentous. Aflaq's wing carried the vote, formally re-establishing the Syrian branch of the party, rejecting both secessionism and immediate reunion with Egypt and, most importantly, expelling the members who opposed Aflaq, al-Bitar and unionism--a direct blow at Hawrani and others who, although not belonging to any cohesive group, were collectively called 'Regionalists' (Qutriyyun), because of the Regional Organization (tanzim qutri) which they had set up apart from the National Command after the secession. These groups held a counter-congress about the same time as the Fifth National Congress was meeting and elected their own Regional Command; on 18 June 1962 Hawrani announced the re-establishment of the Ba'th, thus claiming that the Regionalists were the legitimate Ba'thists.[18]

By this time the Ba'th had split into four distinct and virtually separate parties: the Aflaq al-Bitar wing; Sami Sufan's Socialist Union Movement; the Hawranists; and the other Regionalists. The first two groups were generally identified as anti-secessionists, the latter as supporting both the secession and the existing political regime in Syria. In addition to these groups there were various ex-Ba'thists formally unattached to any of the four factions but generally considered close to the party. These individuals formed a very loosely affiliated 'think-tank' in association with some ex-members of the Syrian Communist Party. Their chief importance lay in their introduction of Marxist elements into Ba'thist ideology and dialectics.[19]

With this visible fragmentation of the Ba'th, Cairo's propaganda attack on the Aflaq wing relented. Aflaq and al-Bitar began sounding almost like Nasir in their statements on Syrian affairs. According to one source, Tabitha Petran, an American journalist long resident in the Arab world, this profound closeness to Nasir stemmed from the Aflaq faction's involvement in an Egyptian plot aimed at overthrowing the Damascus government and installing al-Bitar as premier. This plot was organized from Beirut and scheduled for the nights of 28-29 July, but was uncovered and came to naught.[20]

The regime's reaction to these maneuvers was to accuse Egypt of meddling in internal Syrian affairs. Its representatives at the Shtaura (Lebanon) conference of the League of Arab States brought formal charges against Egypt, which was still calling itself the UAR. The Syrians also accused Egypt of conspiring with the United States to eliminate the Palestinian refugee problem by neglecting the Palestinians. Egypt walked out of the conference, threatening to withdraw from the League; the session adjourned in disarray but remained legally open until the March 1963 Cairo conference voted to remove all mention of the Shtaura conference from the official records of the League.[21]

Events continued in this vein until 8 February 1963, when, as has happened so often in Syria, an external event influenced both the Ba'th and Syria. On that day the Iraqi branch of the Ba'th party seized power in Baghdad which had formerly supported Damascus against Cairo. But this support no longer was to be forthcoming. The new Iraqi strongmen, Abd al-Salam Arif and Abd al-Rahman Arif among others, went to Cairo later in February to join Nasir in celebrating the anniversary of the founding of the UAR. Understandably, the Damascus regime felt surrounded by political enemies. For the most part, his situation engendered a 'let's-stick-together-in-times-of-crisis' feeling in Syria; but it did motivate some senior officers to contact and join in an already-planned coup plot, the moving force of which was Major Ziyad al-Hariri, the commander of Syrian forces on the Israeli front and the brother-in-law of Akram Hawrani. This coup was scheduled for 7 March, but Hariri called it off, explaining that the plans had become known. He then informed the Ba'th that he was going ahead with the coup on 8 March.   He received help from several Ba'th officers who, though few in number, had the cohesive organization of the 'Military Committee' and a political party behind them.   The coup was successful, and al-Hariri asked al-Bitar to form a government.   The Ba'th party was in power.[22]

Chapter IV

TRADITIONAL SYRIA BEFORE THE BA'TH: THE SOCIAL STRUCTURE

Before discussing the Ba'th in power we shall first discuss some of the problems that the Ba'th faced in their efforts to mobilize the support, especially in the countryside, which enabled them to seize power. For, in many ways, the Ba'th had to undermine the traditional political structure or to seize upon its weaknesses before their propaganda could have an effect on the peasants.

When Aflaq and al-Bitar were formulating the ideology of the Ba'th party, the peasants of Syria were still living a way of life which had changed little since the days of the Ottoman Empire. The countryside was dominated by the cities and the cities controlled the state. The non-existent or meager role of the peasants in the socio-economic life of Syria was imbedded in the traditional political, social and economic conditions of the countryside.

On a political level most of the centers of power were controlled by great urban notable-politicians wielding power through the time honored instruments of landed wealth and patronage. Estates could possess as many as several hundred villages and the villagers were as bound as medieval serfs to the owner. The estate owner assumed virtual control over the destiny of the peasants on his land. He acted toward villages which fell under his influence as a medieval lord of the manor to protect his charges from the government, nomads or other clans with whom they might be feuding. At times politicians bought up land in villages in order to assume the role of patron and arbiter. Vote buying was expensive and the cost was later deducted from the spoils of office.   Most of the positions in education or the religious hierarchy were filled by these same elites which further consolidated their political control.   Attempts to gain political power through organization or appeal to issues were non-existent.

Peasants remained on the periphery of the political system.   They regarded government as a threat to them, either asking for more taxes than they could pay or conscripting sons whom the peasants did not want to leave the village.   The peasants lacked political consciousness, had no idea of the importance or implications of national issues and even when they did, they had no re-sources to implement them.   Furthermore, they were divided among themselves and were oriented towards local conflicts and solidarities.

During the first half of the twentieth cen-tury, Syria possessed a 'patrimonial' political structure.   The French during their period of mandate (1920-1946), for reasons of colonial con-trol, perpetuated the patrimonial politics of the nineteenth century.   A 'patrimonial' state is characterized by urban dominance over the rural sector.   This situation is accompanied by the rural masses being fragmented into a mosaic of self-contained units – rural families, clans, tribes, sects and villages.   Historically Syria had been a crossroads of cultural and ethnic influ-ences and an incubator for rival religions and creeds, the remnants of which still remain due largely to the rugged terrain and lack of good communications.   The millet system, by which the Ottomans ruled the non-Muslims in Syria was based on some autonomy for different religious units which further prevented a decrease in or assimilation of the numerous sects.   Division into rival groups was constantly reinforced by the penetration and settlement of nomadic tribes. The practice of endogamous marriage (the custom of marrying within one's own social group or clan) further limited social interchange. Subsistence level agriculture, the lack of markets for commodities and labor, and the primitive nature of roads, telegraph and telephone systems further increased the isolation of the village.

Outside of clan and village the individual had no social existence. His status was determined by membership in his own particular group. He participated in the struggles of his group against rivals for the needed resources of water, land, and house. Patriarchal heads of groups or segments acted as 'gatekeepers' between the locals and the larger political and social groupings. These patron-client relationships were one of the few links between village and urban areas. While villages and clans offered a face of solidarity to the world, internally they were racked by conflict. This kind of social structure was marked by a high level of kin, sectarian and local conflict exacerbated by an environment of extreme scarcity. These tendencies resulted in an 'ardent particularism,' a kind of 'moral familis' expressed by the folk saying: "I against my brother; i and my brother against my cousins; I, my brother and cousins against the world."[2] The ethnic mosaic of rural Syria produced a rich and vigorous community life.

The inability of the rural masses to organize politically made them vulnerable to the economic forces of the cities which controlled the land and the agricultural markets. In Syria, as in so many parts of the third world, the control and cultivation of land were separated from each other. The situation is aptly described in the saying: "He who owns does not work, and he who works does not own."

Distribution of land was marked by concentration of property in great estates owned by the urban notable elites. Even the bulk of medium and small properties were owned by the urban middle class or rural petty bourgeoisie who did not personally cultivate them. Up to the 1950's more than two-thirds of the peasantry were landless. Only in mountainous regions inaccessible to the urban notable and the nomad or in areas where irrigated viniculture (growing of grapes) required patient, individual care, could small owner-cultivators survive. Peasants with small holdings were unable to keep their land in the regions comprising a good deal of the arable land where irregular rainfall forced them to seek credit from landlords or merchants in lean years. They also were sometimes forced to abandon their lands in face of bedouin raids, urban encroachment or local feuding. It was a small step from protection, to patronage and to proprietorship. Many peasants who did own property found it economically useless because of its small size and undesirable location. Peasants were seldom allowed to keep any surplus they might produce. This condition prevented them from accumulating reserves against a bad year or as collateral for a bank loan. As a result, most peasants were dependent on an urban merchant to provide seed and tools needed for planting and harvesting. These merchants relieved the peasants of their crops when the prices were depressed and forced him to seek credit when the interest rates were highest.

The majority of peasants were sharecroppers working on great landed estates. The typical agreement between the owner and the peasant provided that the peasant received 50% of the crops if he supplied water, seeds, implements, and animals, and 25% if he provided only labor.

In garden culture which required a bond of interest between owner and cultivator contracts were more favorable, and, at the other extreme, if labor was excessively plentiful, peasant shares might be reduced to as little as 16%. Peasants were often obliged to render personal services to the lord, such as free labor on his estate (corvee), and for the estate household, provision of food and their daughters as domestic help . In some areas, the lords adopted the practice of periodically expelling sharecroppers to avoid the development of peasant solidarity against them. Most insecure of all were the landless laborers migrating in search of work and entitled to only 1/12 to 1/16 of their work at harvest time. Naturally, these various patterns of tenancy and credit resulted in a highly unequal distribution of agriculture revenue, estimated as follows:

Table I

Population	(8,000,000)
Revenue	
2%	50%
18%	25%
80%	25%

In addition, the landlord was the dominant power in the village, with the local police normally at his disposal. He was, at once, ruler and judge.

In general, most observers believe that apart from garden areas there was little relationship of any kind between owner and peasant. It was less an exchange of services than an expropriation by

the landlord of the producer's surplus as rent for
a monopolized factor of production. The landlord
typically regarded the peasant as a source of in-
come and power. A great cultural gap separated
the two social groups. The landlord played little
role in the agricultural cycle, preferring the
sharecropping tenure precisely because it yielded
revenue without necessitating a substantial contribution of investment or management. The peasant had neither the means nor the motivation to
improve production: the landlord took any surplus, which combined with the instability of dry
farming, prevented the peasant from accumulating
any capital for investment. Reduced to complete
dependency, ignorance, and a subsistence level
existence at best, the peasant's attitude was
essentially fatalistic. The resulting low level
of productivity and no-growth production tended to
relate lord and peasant in a zero-sum game; the
landlord, always short of cash, sought to squeeze
the peasant; the peasant responded with poor working habits, evasion, theft and occasional mutiny.
The consequences of this system were agricultural
stagnation and the reduction of the great mass of
the peasantry to misery and poverty.

     In this way the control of politics and the
state by great notable families, social fragmentation, low political consciousness and extreme
economic dependency of the rural masses, all
seemed to constitute a stable base for the continuation of traditional rule in the years immediately after independence. But the costs of this
system turned out to be too high and contributed
to its ultimate ruin. Under it, the state remained a fragile creature of landed elites. This
condition, combined with the absence of a tradition of an authoritative state, truncated boundaries, the centrifugal segmented social structure
and the political passivity of the masses deprived

those who controlled the government of the loyalties and active energies of the great bulk of the
population. Great social and economic gaps, the
particularistic culture generated by segmentation,
and the low level of integration made development
of a nation with public concerns difficult. The
new state and its traditional elite were themselves incapable of mobilizing the power needed to
respond to the social crises and national threats
the country would soon face. This structural
weakness in turn exposed the state to a takeover
by a political party, such as the Ba'th which made
an especially strong appeal to rural regions and
social issues.

THE EROSION OF THE TRADITIONAL REGIME

There were many factors contributing to the
erosion of the traditional elite other than the
propaganda of the Ba'th party. One of the main
factors contributing to this erosion was the new
social mobility made possible by the capital that
various sectors of the Syrian elite had managed to
accumulate during World War II. The sale of wheat
to allied forces, particularly in Egypt, had been
lucrative. High postwar prices for agricultural
accommodities assured this advantage for several
years. The economic upturn also gave impetus and
provided the necessary capital for the opening of
virgin fields, especially in the north and east,
to the plow.
Independence also created new opportunities
in the newly created army and bureaucracy. Both
institutions in turn generated a great need for
education. A rapid increase in the growth of
population put further pressure on the land which
resulted in greater rural migration to the cities.
In the Latakia and Suwayda (Jabal al-Druze) areas,

inhabited respectively by the minorities of Alawites and Druzes, large numbers of young people
sought new opportunities as officers and teachers-
two professions which they felt would give them
equal prestige with the Sunnis of the urban centers. The long periods away from home necessi-
tated by military training or higher education
served to weaken the grip of the father, family
and all patriarchal forces of control.

The demands raised by the new social forces
could not be met by the traditional elite and led
to insolvable problems. First, social mobilization created in the new groups a strong receptivi-
ty for nationalism, but with the disaster in
Palestine in 1948 , this nationalism appeared as
resentment against the traditional elite for permitting a Zionist victory.[3] The defeat in Palestine created an intense desire for a strong nationally mobilized state capable of acting in the
Arab national cause. The new nationally conscious
groups knew that the traditional elite would be
incapable of achieving this goal. Second, social
mobilization produced rising demands for modern
careers and incomes which by the mid-fifties out-
ran the capacity of the system. Much of the new
wealth created by the war remained in the hands of
a wealthy few. This situation was exacerbated by
the recession in the 1950's, largely caused by a
decline in agricultural production.

Much of the agriculture boom of the late
forties and early fifties was a result of the
exploitation of new lands, not a modernization of
the traditional agriculture sector. The contradictions of the false agricultural boom soon
became evident. As in Turkey, Syria had also
received better than average rainfall up to the
mid-fifties.

Throughout the fifties the Ba'th party was
the main force which tried to mobilize the coun-

tryside (al-Rif). The young students, many from the minorities in the provinces, were the main targets and purveyors of change. The mobilization of the peasants had begun in earnest by Akram Hourani in the early fifties around Hama. After merging with Hourani's party in 1953, the Ba'th continued and expanded its efforts.

The mobilization of peasants was curtailed by the creation of the UAR in 1958. Nasir and his adherents harassed the party. Ba'th leaders as noted above, disagreed on policies to deal with Nasir which led to further splits. The Nasirists themselves advocated rural agrarian reforms which undercut the party's program by lessening the peasants discontent. In the opinion of a leading authority on the Ba'th, Professor Raymond Hinnebusch, the coup d'etat of 1963 was carried out by army officers of rural but petit bourgeois origin and not by leaders of peasants because the Nasirists had eliminated much peasant discontent. The dissolution of the UAR in Syria, in this regard, had a significant impact on the subsequent political development of Syria. The most notable difference was the increased estrangement between the military and civilian elements within the Ba'th. In a word, the army became more difficult to control; prestige lay with the victor. In spite of the conflict between the civilians and the officers, the officers did represent the political mobilization spearheaded by the Ba'th which had occurred during the fifties. This fact precludes considering the 1963 coup simply as a military coup representing only superficial changes among the governing elites. The army officers in many instances were supported by teachers in the provinces. In this light the 1963 coup can be seen as the continuation of the political mobilization of the fifties which was held in abeyance during the period of the UAR. The party rejuvenated itself between 1961 and 1963 and was able to come to power by a coup in 1963. It is understandable that the new leaders, dubbed the Neo-Ba'th, felt keenly the debilitation of the party during the period 1958-63 and that they would be consistently less pan-Arab than the original Ba'th. They were to be more 'Syrian,' indeed, pan-Syrian.

As mentioned above the expansion in grain production was based on the opening of previously unexploited lands in the east which would yield relatively quick returns on modest capital investment. The limits of extensive dry farming of the Jezira section of northeast Syria were soon reached during the dry years of 1958-60, which were accompanied by an astounding 50% drop in production. The poor means of transport between the eastern producing areas and the ports on the Mediterranean also drove up the cost of grain. Meanwhile, international grain prices fell. The farmer was put in the traditional squeeze of rising costs and falling prices. Further, mechanized farming for quick profit was leading to dangerous soil erosion and exhaustion. The same problem was encountered in cotton production where small pumps were used to irrigate, but, without proper drainage, a rise in soil salinity resulted. In the words of one writer, "The land boom was doomed to peter out without continuing into an industrial process for the simple reason that the country did not then possess an infrastructure sufficiently developed for modern industry."[4] Unfortunately the social mobilization generated, in part, by the agricultural expansion had created new needs and demands which had to be met. The question was how to do so.

THE RURAL POLICY OF THE BA'TH

The Ba'th seizure of power in 1963 opened the way for revolutionary changes in Syria. This can be seen partially as a reaction of the villages against centuries of domination by the urban notable class, and an attempt to transform the structure on which the old regime was based.

The 1963 Ba'th regime originated among the rural intelligentsia. Although rural elements would share power for three years with the historical Damascene founders of the party, the more powerful personalities and the majority of the military and civilian partisans were drawn from the provinces, notably Latakia, Dar'a al-Suwayda, and Dayr al-Zawr. They represented the second generation of leadership, drawn from the early core of Ba'thist recruitment among rurals. Owing to the Ba'th's conflicts with Nasir, it had lost a good part of its base among the urban sector, elements of which had supported Nasir. As a result, few urban personalities emerged among the top party elite.

In spite of identification with social origins, Ba'th policies have not been inspired explicitly or predominantly by rural needs. They have revolved largely around the broader issues of Palestine, Arab unity, socialist revolution, the creation of a strong state and the modernization of Syrian society. These policies have had the effect of benefitting rural people for whom opportunities have been opened up and who are being drawn into participation in the political process. Redistribution of wealth has come at the expense of patriarchal urban interests and urban folk have felt most deprived of opportunities for political participation by Ba'th rule. This constraint on choices can be seen in the Ba'th tendency to rely most heavily on development of a rural support

base, owing to the concentration of its traditional and middle class rivals in the cities. In addition to these factors, rural resentment against
the city, urban contempt for village upstarts of
different religious creeds and the belief of many
city folk that they were discriminated against by
the regime, injected an added element of strain
into the Ba'th's relations with the urban population at least until the rise of Hafiz al-Asad to
leadership in 1970.

Can the Ba'th be said to represent a particular stratum of the rural population--e.g., the
minorities, especially Alawites and Druze or the
rural petty bourgeoisie as some have suggested?
Insofar as social origins offer useful explanations, these two groups are well represented. As
regards the minorities, many Syrians do perceive
the regime as a minority, particularly Alawite,
regime. Their beliefs cannot be dismissed as
having no foundation. The current regime has been
referred to as 'adis,' which literally means
lentils, with connotations of rusticity or
'country-bumpkins' and can also be taken as an
anagram of city contempt for Alawite-Druze-
Isma'ili. For historical and political reasons
already discussed and mentioned further below,
minorities were disproportionately represented in
the party and army and have now secured privileged
access to government jobs and favors. In addition, sectarian solidarity has been a significant
factor in intra-regime conflict. Most evidence
seems to indicate that party leaders of minority
origin have not pursued particularistic policies
meant to favor their own sectarian groups, at
least up to 1975. They have not identified
strongly with religion and have not tried ideolog-
ically to turn the party into a sectarian in-
group; although some people contend this was no
longer true by the mid-1970's. Most party members

are not minority members and Sunnis are represented at the top levels, although not as much as they
feel they should be.

Is the Ba'th regime derived from and partial
to rich peasants and the rural petty bourgeoisie
of the 1960's? As regards origin, the senior
leaders of the Ba'th tend to be drawn from those
peasant families who were first able to get a high
school education for their sons. This group does
not appear to have been limited, by any means, to
rich peasants, and, indeed, stems from the main-
stream of middle level peasantry. It does seem
that the most deprived peasants had less chance to
secure education and pursue political opportunities. These historical patterns are reflected to
some degree in the social composition of the party. But it is also true that subsequent recruitment drives have reached deeply into the lower
strata. As regards regime policies, they have
not, it is true, damaged the interests of the
rural petty bourgeoisie. In fact in the 1960's
and 1970's this group was rising dramatically.
Through their reduction or elimination of great
landlords and the slowness of rural re-organization, the party may have actually opened up many
new opportunities for the rural bourgeoisie to
enrich themselves. Furthermore, the regime appears to have done little to help the poorest
landless peasants who often work for the richer
landed peasants. This is probably more a matter
of limited capacity than intention. Nevertheless,
the main thrust of Ba'th rural policy has aimed at
bolstering the small and middle peasants in order
to increase their independence of landlords with
the aim of forging them into a firm base of regime
support. These objectives do not allow one to
dismiss the Ba'th, at least up to the middle of
the 1970's, as a 'petty bourgeois' regime. By the
latter 1970's, however, the regime's policies

began to favor the more capitalistic farmers.

IMPLEMENTATION OF BA'TH RURAL POLICY

What has been the pattern of Ba'th rural policy? The agrarian policy of the Ba'th developed over the years can best be seen as a response to four factors: fairly stable ideological preferences; changing local constraints; opportunities connected with maintenance of central power and solving problems with scarce resources. In the following discussion stable elements of policy will be identified followed by an analysis of policy development in a context of political conflict and structural change.

The basic strategy of Ba'th rural policy has been to break the social and political power of the traditional elite by destroying its monopolistic control over land and markets. This tactic in turn would destroy much of their political control acquired through patronage and peasant dependency. Second, it has sought to mobilize and organize a peasant base of support, to generate legitimacy for party rule and to stimulate peasant participation and cooperation in regime efforts at reform and development. Third, the regime wants to integrate the Syrian state and society by drawing the rural sector into political and social participation. This would reduce the centrifugal effects of the segmental social structure and open up opportunities for rural young people. It would provide a more equitable and rational distribution of power and resources between urban and rural sectors. Fourth, in the villages, it would create a set of modern social institutions and foster the emergence of a socially independent peasantry. Fifth, an effort has been made to stimulate eco-

nomic development in rural areas as a part of the
balanced development of the economy as a whole.
How have these policies developed and how have
they worked out in practice?

The ideological roots of Ba'thist rural
policy can be traced to the sixth National Congress held in the first year of the new regime.
This congress clarified the ideological preferences of the party and defined a body of doctrine
with long range goals. A number of these objectives are of particular relevance to rural policy.

It was announced that the party should create 'popular democracy.' This entails the creation
of a strong party apparatus, penetrating all sectors of society and linking the rural bases to the
urban political center. The function of the party
apparatus is popular organization and mobilization
aimed at cutting the masses off from traditional
influence. Each sector is to participate through
mass political organizations under party leadership and thereby constitute an institutionalized
presence of the masses in the system.

It was decided that the party would undertake
a socialist transformation in the countryside.
The slogan, 'The land to those who till it, and to
each according to his effort,' suggested land
reform. The call for socialist productive relationships implied some form of cooperative or
collective organization of the rural population.
The dominance of the left in this congress is seen
in the assertion that the ultimate form of socialist ownership should be collective farms.
This would stifle the emergence of a rural petty
bourgeoisie dominating poor peasants and would
prevent land fragmentation, facilitate economies
of scale, state planning and resource mobilization. These goals were to rescue the peasant from
his isolation and historic individualism.

The government would aim to equalize the

distribution of wealth, services and opportunity
between city and country.   This would redress
rural grievances ranging from no food to favoritism of one region over another.   Finally, the
Congress declared its belief that a modernizing
agrarian revolution was the key to the general
modernization of Syria.   In 1963 and 1964 these
radical and long-range goals may not have seemed
of immediate relevance to the reality of Ba'th
rule in Syria.   At that time, the party was a
relatively small group of intellectuals and army
officers with a precarious hold on power.   The
regime was in conflict with the Nasirites, other
non-Ba'thist 'progressives,' as well as the upper
classes and the Sunni religious establishment over
its policies and its drive to single party rule.
The Ba'th found itself isolated and on the defen-
sive in Syria's cities.   Its potential rural support was scattered and unorganized; its enemies
were concentrated and mobilized.   In addition,
throughout 1964, the party was divided internally
between its moderate leaders and rural radicals.
This conflict was essentially over policy towards
the urban opposition which the radicals believed
to be bankrupt and with whom the moderates sought
some accommodation.   It is possible to see in the
resolutions of the Congress the outline of a two-
pronged strategy by which the party hoped to break
out of its isolation, outflank its rivals, link up
with the masses and thereby build political power.
The key to winning the masses, party leaders pro-
fessed to believe, was socialist change on a democratic basis with the participation of the masses.
In other words, socialist transformation would
serve to benefit the masses and build support
among them, thus creating opportunities for the
party to bring them into organized public life
under its leadership.   It was no incidental matter
that the radicals intended to take the initiative

in this process in order to undermine their rivals in the party who were less anxious to antagonize the land-owning classes at a time of precarious party rule.

On a practical level, while the party in 1964 was far from having the capacity to 'replace feudal-capitalist with socialist production,' it was able to press ahead with efforts to dismantle the old system. Thus, the first land reform was accelerated and a new, more radical reform promulgated. The new reform, the most radical in the Middle East, halved the ownership ceilings specified in the 1958 reform, from 80 hectares of irrigated land to 40 and from 300 hectares of non-irrigated land to 150. The first reform had begun the process of demolishing the interests of the large magnates. The second reform reduced further their control of land and also struck at medium-sized landlords. Party leaders hoped that the two reforms would provide the basis for a socialist agrarian structure, serve as a focus for the mobilization of peasant support, undermine the influence and control of the landlords, raise the living standards in the country and help create an independent peasantry. Supplementing the reform was a radicalized agrarian relations law designed to protect peasant rights by regulating equitably the relations of owners and investors with the labor force and providing for major increases in the share of production allotted to the laborers.

At the same time organizational drives were initiated in the towns and countryside. Beginning in late 1964, the party created special sub-branches charged with recruitment in each of the sectors believed to be part of the party's natural mass base of peasants, workers and students. At the same time, the foundations of the General Federation of Peasants were laid. In 1964 local party organizations began to set up village committees, concentrating on areas where peasants were benefitting from the land reform. Late the same year party branches began submitting the names of candidates to man a skeleton union hierarchy at the provincial and central levels. The fledgling union encountered such problems as the infiltration of the cadres by traditional leaders and rich peasants. As a result, the party had to construct the union under close supervision. Despite these obstacles, by September 1965, the union held its first congress as a training session for the first batch of peasant cadres.

From the preceding account, it should be clear to the reader that by the mid-1960's and early 1970's under the leadership of the Ba'th, Syria had a 'mobilized' political structure which had evolved considerably from the 'patrimonial' system described in the first part of this survey. At this point it is appropriate to look closely at the mobilization system. A mobilized political structure in many ways characterized the changes which began taking place in 1949 and which obtained in the 1970's in Syria. Changes were particularly rapid after 1963 under Ba'thist rule.

CHARACTERISTICS OF A 'MOBILIZATION' POLITICAL SYSTEM

A mobilization system is a political order in which the generation and consolidation of political power in the hands of a small and cohesive national leadership group is achieved with a view toward changing society in a radical fashion, unrestrained by legal controls or constitutional considerations. Leaders in this type of system encourage mass participation in the process of social transformation at the level of application rather than legislation. It is a political system

in which political legitimacy is derived largely
from ideology and personal appeal of the leader,
often enforced by plebiscite. The leadership is
revolutionary in the sense that top leaders
achieve political power by seizure, be it military
coup d'etat or armed national struggle. Political
positions are most often, as in the case of a mon-
archical or patrimonial system, filled by co-
optation. Sometimes they are formalized by popular
elections. Co-optation in political and administrative positions is based on defined ideology and
on skill and ability to serve.

In a mobilizational system the articulation
and dissemination of official ideology is a focal
point of the regime and deliberate efforts are
made to enlist intellectuals in the service of the
regime's indoctrination policy. The regime's
ideology tends to be abolitionist in the sense
that it rejects, almost totally, established political institutions and former political ideologies. It is also often or, at least, professes
to be egalitarian and populist in nature. It
fosters or claims to foster the interest of the
masses for support. The masses occupy a central
position in the formal ideology of the regime,
though not in the making of policy. It is also
nationalistic and collective in conscience in the
sense that it stresses the place of the nation at
the expense of the individual. Conformity to
official ideology is required from citizens.

Mobilizational politics concentrates policy
in the hands of the leader and his cohorts with
the aid of technocrats enlisted in the service of
the regime and it is explicit that modernization
assumes a predominant role in the outlook of the
regime. It is conceived in ideological terms as
the re-organization of national authority and the
concentration of powers in the hands of the national leader to give the capacity to introduce

necessary change.   Modernization is viewed therefore as a comprehensive process in which not only
does society respond to challenges of the world
environment by adopting technical innovation, the
establishment of industry and the elevation of
science in the educational system, but also by the
re-education or indoctrination of the individual
with new political values and ideas and the re-
shaping of political and economic relations in
society.

As in the case of the adaptive patrimonial
system, the bureaucracy develops into a large body
subservient to the regime and serving as its main
instrument of social change.   Access to official
employment at various levels opens up widely as a
result of the expanded governmental role in the
economic and social fields, a process which con-
tributes to social mobility.   Political participation takes generally the form of acclamation,
whether in mass rallies, demonstrations of support
or election through plebiscite.   It is competitive
within circumscribed limits defined by the regime's leaders in party elections and elections to
the legislative assembly .   However, at the level
of local government it is relatively free and
takes the form of electing leaders to manage local
affairs, a process encouraged by national leaders
as a means to stimulate locals to cooperate and
bear their share in the implementation of the
government's developmental policy.   The mobilized
regime organizes mass support in a single political movement to the exclusion of all others.   The
movement is led and patronized by the regime's
leaders.

As in the case of a patrimonial regime,
unchecked use of coercion prevails if the regime
is challenged or threatened in any way.   Thus the
political freedom of the individual is seriously
compromised.   This   is   because   a   mobilization

regime has a low tolerance point toward political opposition or the existence of$_5$ organized groups free from government regulation.

The Ba'th in Syria after 1963 exhibited all or a composite of the twelve or so characteristics of a mobilization political system which I have just discussed above, but by 1976 as a result of the complications arising from intervention in Lebanon, the 'mobilizational' aspects of the Ba'th regime had begun to deteriorate seriously. This was true particularly in the reduction of the Ba'th's popular appeal and its decreased support from the masses, especially among the Sunni's. The pan-Syrianess of Ba'thism, let alone its pan-Arabism, became to be more characterized as merely pan-Alawiism. This became more true in the late 1970's as the 'Islamic Opposition' gathered force. The increasing opposition to al-Asad's regime reduced the appeal of Ba'thism as a 'comprehensive' modernizing ideology. After 1975 political participation grew even more limited and the recruitment bases of the party diminished. These trends were accompanied by greater coercion and by 1978 the government was engaged consistently in quelling serious revolts.

The opposition to Syria's intervention in Lebanon served as a catalyst for increased opposition at home so that by 1978 al-Asad's government began to resemble, in several aspects, the patrimonial system which it had replaced some fifteen years previously. The major difference being that the regime in 1978 was composed of a political elite of an ethnic, religious and geographically peripheral group rather than a Sunni political elite. This was true particularly in that the top political leadership of the government and the party now remained in the hands of a relatively small and specific group which stressed personal and natural ties such as kinship, ethnic, reli-

gious and tribal loyalties. Also, the articulation and use of political ideas to influence
public opinion lessened. Out and out coercion
replaced tradition, culture and religion as
principles of social control. Increasingly, post-
1976 Syrian society became more divided and
segmented further into ethnic, religious and
status groups. As al-Asad's regime became more
embattled the decision-making elite group was
narrowed. The gap between the needs of the al-Asad
regime for survival militated against not only
political development but economic development as
well. The isolation of the Syrian regime from
Iraq and Jordan increased in 1979 when al-Asad,
desperately attempting to break his isolation,
made a tactical alliance with Mu'ammar al-Qaddafi
of Libya and then by recognizing the Islamic
Republic regime of Ayatollah Khomeini in Iran.
Al-Asad persisted in his support for Iran even
after war broke out between that country and Iraq
in September, 1980. As a result of Syria's support for Iran, Iraq and Jordan overtly began to
support al-Asad's opposition in Syria. By 1980
Syria was further isolated in the Arab world.
Unable to extricate itself from Lebanon and faced
with a belligerent Israel al-Asad was able to do
nothing effective against Israel when it annexed
the Golan Heights on 14 December, 1981. The Ba'th
regime had become politically and diplomatically
embattled.

63

Chapter V

THE ROLE OF THE MINORITIES IN THE BA'TH: ALAWITES, DRUZES, ISMA'ILIS

Several places in this study we have alluded to the role of minorities in the evolution of the Ba'th party and its ideology. Michel Aflaq's attitude toward the Kurds has already been mentioned. More important than the Kurds and Isma'ilis have been the Alawites and Druzes. The Alawites and Druzes, although Muslim, are the two major religious groups who do not follow the Sunnite faith. In the 1938 Syrian census these two groups totaled 280,000 out of a total population of about two and a half million, or slightly more than ten percent.

Although products of Arab civilization, and members of heterodox Islamic sects, these two groups developed over time certain identities and characteristics that set them apart and isolated them from the Syrian population.[1] Their history was fraught with clashes and tensions with the Sunnis on political and social levels. During the period of the Ottoman Empire (1516-1918) and the French Mandate (1920-1945), as well as after independence, the Druzes and Alawites fought attempts by the central government to control them and at times even challenged central authority. To understand the frequent challenge of these minorities to their respective overlords - Sunni Arab, Ottomans, French and independent governments - a brief history of each is in order.

The Druzes

The Druzes have two names: The Druze, derived from Muhammad Ibn Isma'il al-Darazi, and al-Muwahhidin which reflects their fundamental belief in "one and only one God."

The Druzes are located in three countries: in Syria (Hawran or Jabal al-Druz), in Lebanon (Mount Lebanon--Shuf and Aley; south Lebanon--Hasbaya, and Biqa'-Rashaya), and in Israel (Mount Hermon, western Galilee and Mount Carmel). There are small numbers of communities in Jabal al-Ala near Aleppo, around Damascus, the Golan Heights and Beirut.

Opinions differ as to the origins of the Druze community. Some scholars believe that they are of Persian origin; others, that they are of Arab origin from Yemen or of Aramaic peasant origin. There is no solid evidence to support any of these arguments. The Druzes, however, consider themselves to be Arabs and the non-Druze Arabs also consider them Arabs but not Muslims. They have a long history and have lived under a number of dynasties. Their desire to retain their religious and cultural identity, as well as the secretive nature of their system, led to a series of clashes with the central authorities in successful attempts to retain their separate status.

The Druzes trace their origins back to the sixth Fatimid Caliph, al-Hakim (966-1021). Al-Hakim declared himself to be the last incarnation of God and Muhammad ibn Isma'il al-Darazi tried to propagate this message in Cairo. As a result of this unusual call, both al-Darazi and al-Hakim were allegedly murdered. Since then, and probably because of the radical departure from orthodox beliefs, all doctrines, beliefs and rituals have remained a closed book, opened only gradually to the initiated ones and no attempts have been made to gain new converts.

There are four articles or principles to which the Druzes adhere: the concept of the universality of God; belief in the deification of the Fatimid Caliph al-Hakim; belief in the five divine ministers and the three secondary ministers each of whom represents a specific theological concept. Finally there are seven composed precepts which constitute a moral code. The Druzes also hold to the doctrine of transmigration of souls and they are monogamous.

It has long been debated whether the Druzes are indeed Muslims at all. The Druzes do not follow or accept the five Pillars of Islam and they conduct their religious affairs according to a code quite separate from other Muslim sects. If we consider these factors it may be concluded that the Druzes can be considered peripheral Muslims. This is the view of non-Druze Muslims especially.

The Druze religious organization consists of a formal principal or head and a number of officials who deal with religious matters and personal status law. The Druze community is divided into two classes: The 'Uqqal or intelligentsia, and the Juhal or those in ignorance.

The Druzes in Syria follow the Law of Personal Status which was drawn up by the Lebanese Druzes in 1948. It subsequently was adopted in Syria in 1953 and in Israel in 1961. This law includes matters involving inheritance, marriage, divorce, protection of children and other matters.

THE ALAWITES

The original name of this group was Nusayri, derived from the word Nazerini, a local tribe known in the Roman period. Others have suggested that it is derived from Ibn Nusair, an Isma'ili who lived about the end of the ninth century. Their name, Alawite, reflects one of their basic religious doctrines, the deification of

Ali, the son-in-law and paternal nephew of Muhammad. Although little is known about their
religion, they are considerably removed from
orthodox Islam and Shi'ism in their religious
convictions and beliefs. They have a sacred book
called Majmu' and their creed is a mixture of
extravagant peripheral Shi'ite and Islamic doctrines and ancient pagan beliefs, including the
doctrine of transmigration.

The Alawites, who were usually farmers
living in a state of constant poverty and need,
follow religious leaders or shaykhs who control
their social and religious lives. Ali, the nephew
of the Prophet Muhammad, occupies a central and
cardinal place in their religion. They believe in
one God who manifested himself to the world
seven different times and that Ali is the greatest
and most important manifestation of God. Ali's
humanity was only apparent, since he was made
of flesh and blood but he did not act like
ordinary humans.

The Alawite religion, as with Islamic faith,
generally has no ordained clergy. Their shaykhs
are, however, in addition to their role as religious leaders of the community, responsible for
matters pertaining to personal status and waqf or
religious endowments.

The Alawite community has passed through a
number of significant phases. They lived in
isolation for centuries in Jabal al-Nusayriyyah
near Latakia. They were able to protect
themselves against a number of invaders and
retain the residues of their culture while
accepting some aspects of their invaders'
patrimony. They converted to Christianity, since
it reflected some of their own beliefs and later
adopted Islam, but they retained part of their
pre-Christian and Islamic cohesion and group
identity.

The majority of the Alawites live in the province of Latakia, but some have spread into the province of Homs and Hama.   Some are located in Acre or Akkar, a Lebanese district, and in some villages to the north of Latakia in Hatay, formerly Alexandretta, today a province of Turkey.   Another small community of Alawites is settled in southern Lebanon at Wadi al-Taym and on the west bank of the Jordan.

In Syria the Alawites are particularly concentrated in three areas: the coast, the mountains and the inland plains.   Although they were conquered by many invaders, they were able to maintain their integrity as a separate community.   The Arab impact was too strong for them to resist, and they gradually adopted Arabic to the detriment of Syriac which was their native tongue.

The crusades marked another chapter in Alawite history.   The Alawites fought the invaders and continued to fight the Muslims, especially the Ottoman rulers who governed them until the arrival of the French.   In the twelfth century, for instance, the Isma'ili's, the Shi'ites who governed Egypt, invaded Alawite territory and dominated this area until the Ottomans took over in 1517 and ruled until World War I.

THE ALAWITES AND DRUZES
UNDER THE OTTOMANS

The Alawites and Druzes played important roles during the Ottoman period.   The Druzes continued to dominate the area in which they lived until the middle of the eighteenth century before succumbing to Maronite rule.   Even after the Maronite assumption of power, however, most Druze families were actually able to develop and establish their own dynastic and local feudal systems, which accepted nominal Ottoman control in return for recognizing the legitimacy of the local Druze leaders.[2]

The first half of the nineteenth century was a period of great importance and historical challenge for the Druzes. They opted for the status quo, choosing to remain loyal to the Ottoman Empire and to align themselves with Great Britain. The latter, for reasons of imperial policy, supported the 'territorial integrity' of the Ottomans. The opponents of the Druzes were the Maronites and their ally, the French, who wished to see the Ottoman Empire split up. Behind these alliances were deeper political and social attitudes. The Maronites, with an increasingly dynamic society in terms of education, trade and agriculture were desirous of more control and increased contact with Europe. The Druzes felt threatened by the same changes and turned inward toward their traditional life. As a result of the above alliances, there were many clashes between the Druzes and Maronites. The role of Ibrahim Pasha (1830-40), the son of Muhammad Ali of Egypt, in Syria added to tensions between the two groups. The hostility created between the Maronites and Druzes during this period was to be a recurrent feature of the politics of the area for years to come. The worst clash came in 1860 when the Druzes, in retaliation for Maronite encroachments on their claimed lands, and with Ottoman and British support, attacked Maronite villages. The 1860 conflict is of immense importance in Middle Eastern history.[3] It consolidated Muslims and Christians along religious lines, papering over with new administrative procedure the differences which existed between the two religions and their respective sects.

During the decline of the Ottoman Empire in the 1880's and 1890's, the Ottoman government's control over the Druzes decreased further. Under the leadership of the al-Atrash family, the Druzes were in constant rebellion against the government in Istanbul. The relations between the Porte and Jabal al-Druze were no better under the Young Turk regime which came to power in 1909. In 1910 the Druzes staged a major revolt against the Young Turk government.

The Alawites were not as prominent as the Druzes in the politics of the Ottoman Empire. They were not even influential enough to be regarded as a millet or a religious group with certain autonomy with regard to communal practices. As a result of Ottoman policy, however, the Alawites were able to practice their own interpretation of Islam. In the 1860's and late 1870's strong Ottoman governors such as Rashid Pasha and Midhat Pasha tried to improve the general conditions of Syrians, including Alawites, but it was a case of too little too late.

The Alawites, like the Druzes, continued their rebellious ways against Turkish rule. Increasingly in the 1880's and 1890's, Alawi intellectuals like their Sunni and Druze counterparts participated in movements supporting autonomy from the Ottoman government. The rule of Abdulhamid II (1878-1908) did little to mitigate the desires for autonomy by the Alawites. The Alawites received little benefit from the centralized and hence, largely 'Sunni' based policies of Abdulhamid II's government. The Alawites continued their rebellions during the era of Young Turk (1909-1918) rule. The Turkification policies pursued by the Young Turks increased the cooperation of the Alawites with the Arab nationalist movement.

THE ALAWITES AND DRUZES
DURING THE MANDATE (1920-1945)

The roles of the Alawites and the Druzes were of particular significance in the Mandate period, especially during the 1920's when they engaged in a series of revolts. These rural revolts were not exclusively Alawite, Druze or Isma'ili. In the Jezira, Sunni nomadic tribesmen also rebelled. Urban politicians used these rural revolts to bring pressure against the French to ease their repressive measures under the mandate. Ironically the revolts did give urban politicians more power vis-a-vis the rural regions. This was an injustice the Alawites and Druzes tried to rectify by participating in the Ba'th party in the 1950's. Many times the goals of the two groups were the same. But because of or in spite of Alawite resistance to the French and because of the French policy of 'divide and rule' among the sects, the Alawites and the Druzes received concessions increasing their autonomy. The Alawites and the Druzes opposed French rule, but they also opposed rule by Sunni Muslims, at whose hands they felt they had suffered so much. As a result, the Alawites revolted in 1919 against the brief rule of King Faysal, who in their opinion represented Sunni interests. The French encouraged the Alawites and supplied them with weapons. This further embittered the Sunnis and other proponents of Arab nationalism. But the Alawites were no mere hirelings of the French. In 1921, after the French had defeated Faysal and expelled him from Syria, the Alawites rebelled in turn against the French. The 1921 rising helped to resurrect the Arab nationalism of the Alawites in the eyes of their detractors, not to mention their own eyes. The Alawites like to point out that the rebellion of the Alawite, Salih al-Ali, in 1919 succeeded in forcing the French out of the northern coastal region of Syria. Moreover, this was accomplished without help from Damascus. In spite of the suppression of the 1921 rebellion by the French, many Syrian historians believe that one of the main consequences of the rebellions of the 1920's was to increase the ties between the rural areas and the larger cities making effective resistance to French rule possible. While this may be true, it should be noted that Alawite motivations for revolt were undoubtedly the desire for autonomy within Syria regardless of who was the ruler. Aware of this feeling the French created and fostered policies to promote separate identities for the Alawites and Druzes. In September 1920 an 'Alawite Territory' was created. In 1930 the Alawite region was given the title of 'Governorate of Latakia.'

Although relations between the Alawites and the Sunni Muslim majority during the early French period were excellent at the level of their common political struggle, social relations were marred by sharp stratification between the two communities. The Alawites of the Latakia region, Homs, Hama, and the coastal area lived in delapidated villages, working as indentured farmers exploited by absentee landlords who were mainly Sunnis/ Christian, or who belonged to the few wealthy Alawite families. The Alawite masses were socially isolated and economically exploited by their landowners who usually lived in towns and came to the village only to collect rents from their estates.

These religious differences, added to the economic gap, increased the polarization and feelings of independence of the mountain people, particularly the Alawites and the Druzes, and, at the same time, increased feelings of social difference and superiority among the urban dwellers.

A small number of Alawites reacted against these labels and stereotypes by expressing their adherence to the Muslim community and Arab nationalism, stressing their Arab identity. Salih al-Ali's revolt in 1921 became their symbol of and contribution to Arab Nationalism. Arab authors, including Alawite scholars, trace Alawite tribal leaders and notables to Arab tribes. Alawite scholars, especially after they became an important factor in Syrian politics, have striven to muster every kind of proof, including manuscripts and even fatawa, or religious legal judgements, that they are true Muslims and firm supporters of Arab Nationalism.

The suppression of the Druzes rebellions of 1919 and 1921 temporarily curtailed Druze unrest. But the effective division of Syria into four zones: Latakia, Damascus, Aleppo, and Jabal al-Druz provided the impetus for a rebellion originating among the Druzes, but which soon reached national proportions. The report of the King-Crane Commission which investigated the preferences of the people of Iraq, Palestine and Syria in an effort to determine jurisdiction in the mandates stated that people preferred an American mandate or, if that were not possible, a British one. The people of $_5$ Syria definitely did not want French overlords. While there is a dispute as to whether the Druzes rebellion of 1925-28 was a sectarian rebellion or a pan-Arab Syrian rebellion, the events of these years did propel the Druzes into the forefront of the struggle which resulted in several significant political changes.

French authorities for imperialistic reasons granted the Druzes a degree of autonomy, especially with regard to their traditions, customs, legal system and social structure. In addition, this policy also provided a better 'autonomous' educational system for the region. There was a second strand of Syrian history developing as an offshoot of the rebellion. Druze leaders, in conjunction with Arab nationalist leaders in Damascus, initiated a series of demands for the inclusion of Jabal al-Druz and Latakia into Syria. As a result, the French bowed to Arab nationalist demands to unite Damascus and Aleppo. Latakia and Jabal al-Druze, however, remained autonomous. These actions indicated cooperation between the minorities and the Arab nationalists but did not suggest that the Druzes, or Alawites wanted total integration. This conclusion is further made clear by other political developments which increased or, at least, sustained the hostility between the minority-dominated rural regions and the Sunni-dominated cities.

The urban politicians became very active and articulate in their demands for political independence. They encouraged demonstrations, urban disturbances, a constitution, elections and independence. A second development which was greatly to influence the rise of the Ba'th was the increased role of students in politics. Students of minority and village origins sent to the city for education became exposed to the currents of nationalism.

Many times urban and rural youth combined in demonstrations against French rule. Insurrections were rampant in the 1920's. Through a variety of devices the French attempted to use the Druzes and Alawites to offset the Arab nationalists in the large cities. From 1933-39 the districts of Aleppo and Damascus made steady political gains, although at some cost, against the obstinate French. Forced by events in Europe and the more 'progressive colonialization' techniques of Britain in Iraq, which had obtained a degree of independence in 1933, the French acceded to some nationalist demands. But this did not stop the French from encouraging separatist movements in Latakia and Jabal al-Druze. In 1938-39 the Druzes, along with the Jezira demanded independence. In 1938 Latakia became virtually independent. These actions were sufficient to put an end to the Nationalist government. When World War II broke out in full force, Syria was again in the tight grip of France under the Vichy regime. The imperialist control of France became considerably looser during the course of the war. In 1943, under British pressure, the Free French who had replaced the Vichy government in Syria during the same year, restored the constitution of Syria. After general elections were held in the summer of 1943, the National Bloc came to power with Shukri al-Quwwatly as President. In 1944 both the United States and USSR recognized Syria, and in 1945 as a result of her declaration of war on Germany, Syria became a member of the United Nations.[6]

After the termination of French rule in 1946, the Druzes and Alawites followed different paths. A large portion continued their traditional ways in a separate political entity. Another group of these minorities became involved in revolutionary movements. A third group, and the one which was to have the most effect on Syrian politics in the 1960's and 1970's, joined the army. The sequence of coup d'etats which plagued the Syrian government in the late forties and early fifties and the subsequent purges of officers served to advance the Alawite and Druze officers in the ranks. Ranked too low to participate in the coups other than in technical ways, they were not subject to the purges which followed each coup, especially the coups of 1949-1954, the internal army conflicts of 1954-58 and the upheaval following the UAR period (1958-1961). This trend was continued in the coups of 1966 and 1970.

It is not surprising that Alawites and Druzes chose the army for a career. As is the case with lower economic groups around the world, especially in third world countries, the army provided the only vehicle of social mobility. The peasants and the minorities were unable, unlike the city dweller, to muster the cash to bribe their way free of the required two years of military service. Rather than a harsh obligation, the villagers looked upon their two years of military service as a release from the work and drudgery of village life. The result was that many Alawites and Druzes, of the mountainous and rural areas became officers. This factor together with religious diversity eventually produced social differences and tension within the army and made it easier for the radical ideological parties to infiltrate the officers' ranks. This situation also admirably fitted the French policy and practice of recruiting troops for its Troupes speciales, the imperial armed forces, from the minorities, especially the Alawites.

Spared the purges of the 1950's and 1960's, the Alawites and Druzes had reached the top ranks by 1963-64. The rise of the Alawites and Druzes in the Army to field and general level officers meant that they would now become involved in the struggle between Salah al-Jadid and Hafiz al-Asad, both Alawites. The struggle between these men intensified when Salah al-Jadid left the army in 1966 to become General Secretary of the party, while al-Asad remained in control of the Armed Forces as Minister of Defense and commander of the Air Force.

The fact that there was in-fighting among Alawites themselves is itself indicative of their dominance by 1966, as we shall see in the next chapter. In fact it was after the February 1966 coup that the collaboration between the Alawite and Druze officers came to an end. Salim Hatum, the Druze chief of the commando units who participated in the coup, felt that the Druzes had not received a fair share of power and tried to mobilize his supporters in the army and party. The years 1966-70 were a period of further purges and dismissals of non-Alawites which included several influential Isma'ili officers as well as Druzes. In the 1960's as non-Alawites left they were replaced by the relatives of Alawite officers. Alawites also began to dominate the rank and file. Some brigades were totally Alawite. An unprecedented development had taken place: a minority, albeit Muslim, began to dominate a largely Sunni state through its control of the military. This development had and continues to have tremendous importance for the modern history of Syria as well as the entire Middle East.[9]

While the Alawites and Druzes were doing well on the military front, they were also successful in politics. Because of their secular outlook, the Ba'th, the SSNP and Communists were more attractive to Alawites and Druzes than the Muslim Brothers, a conservative religious group headquartered in Egypt, that had a largely urban Sunni following. It is true that large numbers of Alawites and Druzes, along with other minorities, joined the army and various political parties for reasons outlined above, but Alawites and Druzes accelerated their participation in political parties and the army as a result of the union with Egypt leading to the formation of the United Arab Republic (UAR) in 1958. This point is noteworthy because the Alawites and particularly the Druzes did not favor union with Egypt. The Alawites, already feeling themselves a minority in Syria, could not be pleased with the addition of a large Sunni population of Egyptions to the Syrian Sunni majority. The planned dissolution of the Ba'th party, along with all Syrian parties, jeopardized the hopes of the rural populations--especially the Druzes and Alawites-- for the social revolution and the reforms they [10] expected the Ba'th to undertake. Accordingly the Alawites were primarily afraid that they were going to be pushed around in favor of Egyptian immigrants and were particularly worried that the land to be reclaimed by the Ghab irrigation project would be turned over to Egyptian peasants.[11]

These fears encouraged the Alawites and Druzes to oppose the UAR and they were glad to see its dissolution in 1961. The Ba'th party made its 'great leap forward' at that time, and one of its instruments was the Ba'th party machine of Latakia which the Alawites controlled. Three years after the Ba'th seized power in 1963 the Alawites extended their control over both the army and the party. As was stressed in the earlier part of this chapter, however, it was not the sectarian policy of the Ba'th that carried it to power, but its attention to the lower socio-economic stratas, minorities, secularism and the agriculture policy that it fashioned to meet their needs. Since the Alawites and the Druzes formed a significant proportion of this strata, they too benefited proportionately from Ba'th policies.

The social and political gains that the Alawites and Druzes began to make in the 1960's were also sustained through education. Educational opportunities for the Alawites were extremely scarce before the social revolution. In

1952, the average number of teachers per thousand students in Latakia was 1.94, while the total average for Syria was 2.56. Despite their poverty, many Alawite men, realizing the importance of education, moved with their families to cities where at least one son was able to attend high school. This desire for education and the willingness to sacrifice for it spread in the 1950's, 1960's and 1970's throughout the countryside of Syria. These educated people became the source of the Alawite and Druze middle class. Aware of the importance of education, Alawites in positions of authority influenced the government to invest considerable sums of money for education in their areas.

Statistics for education (Tables 1 and 2) show that Alawites standards have begun to equal the standards for the whole of Syria.

TABLE I

STUDENTS AND CLASSROOMS
IN LATAKIA PROVINCE AND SYRIA
(1968 figures)

	Syria	Latakia
Average number of students per classroom:		
Primary	25	24
Secondary	42	43
Average number of students per teacher:		
Primary	37	43
Secondary	24	26

Table II

STUDENTS IN LATAKIA AND SYRIA
(1968 Figures)

	Syria		Latakia	
	Number	Percent	Number	Percent
Primary	813,225	100	106,183	13
Secondary	242,947	100	38,169	16
Population	6,244,418	100	429,782	7

Tables I and II are from Hreib, page 167 who quotes from Statistical Abstract 1969-1970 (Damascus: Government Printing Press, 1871) 336-39.

In many ways the pattern of education among the Druzes paralleled that of the Alawites, although by the 1960's Druze advances were not as accelerated as those of the rest of Syria. This trend was partially due to the increased standards of education throughout Syria. It seems clear, however, that the gains made through the army and the Ba'th will be sustained by the schools and universities. Even if the Alawites are toppled from power, it is apparent

that they will continue to play a proportionately
larger share in the politics of Syria than their
numbers indicate, and, assuredly, a much larger
role than they did before 1963.

Chapter VI

THE BA'TH IN POWER; 1963-66

The coup of 1963 became known in Ba'th historiography as the Ba'th Revolution of 8 March 1963 even though participants were largely members of the Military Committee over which the party had no control. The social revolution expressed in Ba'thist thought did not occur.[1] Major Ziad Hairi, the leader of the coup and Akram Hourani's brother-in-law, initially set up an organization called the National Council of the Revolutionary Command (NCRC), which became the supreme administrative authority. The NCRC was composed of ten officers, four independents, three Nasirists and three Ba'thists. Lt.-General Luay al-Atasi, an independent with pro-Ba'th sympathies, was elected president of the council. Plans to add ten civilians to the NCRC were hampered by the Ba'th's insistence that half of these be Ba'thists.[2]

Pro-Nasir demonstrations occurred in many areas of Syria after the coup. They forced Damascus and the Ba'th, which had the predominant position in the new regime, to hold negotiations with the Egyptians and the Iraqis about the possibility of establishing a tripartite union.[3]

In these negotiations Syria and the Ba'th in particular were at a disadvantage. On the one hand there were the intertwined rivalries among and within what can be considered the five major power centers in Syria at that time: the NCRC; the ministry of defense and higher military positions; the governmental structure of the premier and the cabinet; the Ba'th's Syrian Regional Command; and the Ba'th's National Command.[4]

Within the Ba'th itself there were four major conflicts. The first of these was between the

Aflaq-Bitar wing which did not really want a full union, and the younger Ba'th members who wanted to organize 'the masses against reactionary secessionism.' Other conflicts were beginning to materialize at this time. These were between the National Command and the Military Committee; between the National Command and both the Syrian and Iraqi Regional Commands; and between the Syrian Regional Command and the Military Committee.[5]

Nevertheless, Syria went ahead with the Cairo Unity Talks, as the negotiations were called, even though few of the participants actually aspired to unity. These talks were held in three separate stages: trilateral negotiations in five meetings from 14 to 16 March; five Syrian-Egyptian meetings on 19 and 20 March; and ten meetings between 6 and 14 April, of which the first two were again Syrian-Egyptian and the last eight trilateral.[6]

Nothing concrete really emerged from the talks until 19 March when Aflaq and al-Bitar both went to Cairo. It was then that Nasir began putting on a show, taking advantage of the slow, deliberate conversational style of his rivals and the fact that they had come to him to get a new agreement and to stabilize their regime.

Despite this exhibition and after torrents of recrimination, double-talk and contradictions, the three countries signed an agreement on 17 April, under which the president (who would be Nasir, of course) held virtually all power. However, it provided also for a transitional period of five months with 20 additional months before the implementation of full union. Naturally, given such ingredients, the union had little chance of ever coming about and, indeed, it simply died a slow and ignominious death.[7]

While the negotiations were going on, the

Ba'th had moved to consolidate their political position in Syria at the expense of the Nasirists. At the beginning of April, they managed to get the NCRC to condone and conduct a purge of Nasirist officers. Several cabinet ministers resigned in protest, forcing the entire al-Bitar government to resign on 11 May. There then followed some strange maneuvers. Dr. Sami al-Jundi, a former Socialist Union Movement member drawn into the Ba'thist sphere because of family connections with Ba'thists, was asked to form a government. He gave up, telling the NCRC that non-Ba'th politicians had refused to cooperate with him. But at the same time the NCRC apparently sent the minister of education, Dr. Sami al-Drubi, to an educational conference in Cairo, where he consulted with Nasir. When he returned, al-Drubi, a moderate Ba'thist, proposed to several non-Ba'th leaders that he become premier, whereupon he would give them a majority of cabinet posts. When he took this proposal to the Ba'th, they refused to cooperate.[8]

Another version contests this view stating that al-Drubi's candidacy was actually a cover allowing the Ba'thists to say they had tried to negotiate in good faith with the Nasirists, but that the latter would not negotiate reasonably even with a non-Ba'thist.[9]

The outcome of all these maneuvers was that al-Bitar formed another cabinet with 12 of 18 ministries headed by Ba'thists or pro-Ba'th independents. The other six posts remained unfilled because no other groups would participate. While the new government proclaimed its determination to live up to the unity agreement, it was busy imprisoning pro-Nasir newspaper editors and shutting down non-Ba'th publications. In conjunction with this crackdown, Amin al-Hafiz, soon to become a strongman in Syrian

politics,   harshly   put   down   pro-Nasir
demonstrations.[10]

By July the Ba'th was strong enough to oust
Hariri   as   chief-of-staff,   dismissing   30   of   his
supporters   from   the   army   while   he   was   in   Algiers.   On 18 July an attempted Nasirist coup was
fought off.   This coup produced two new elements
into   Syrian   politics: strong   resistance   to   coup
attempts   (the   Ba'th   had   used   tanks,   jets   and
artillery); and summary   execution of coup participants.   That day marked the end of Cairo's and
Damascus's lip   service   to   the   unity   agreement,
but more importantly, the end of organized pro-
Nasir strength in Syria.[11]

Although the Ba'th had consolidated its hold
over Syria,   it was   still   beset   by   internal   difficulties.   Besides the factionalism described above
there   was   a   lack   of   popular   support   for   the   regime.   In an   effort   to   increase   its   popular   base,
the Ba'th opened its membership ranks to many
newcomers.   This   move   had   the   far-reaching
consequences   of   radically   changing   the   social
background of members and making the Aflaq-al-
Bitar   wing   of   the   party   a   minority.   Concurrent
with   these   changes,   there   emerged   a   group   of
young   radical   Ba'thists   which   eventually   included
most   of   the   anti-Aflaq   members   of   the   party,
gathering   support   from   old-line   regulars,   near-
Marxists   and   newly   recruited   proteges   of   the
Military   Committee--the   common   determining
feature   of   which   was   their   opposition   to   the
"Founding Fathers."[12]

By   this   time   the   Military   Committee   had
complete control of the army and heavy representation   in   the   Regional   Command.   With   the   support of the anti-Aflaqists, the Committee also had
virtual   control   of   the   party,   a   control   which   its
members   began   using   to   accomplish   one   of   their
primary   objectives--the   ouster   of   Aflaq   and

al-Bitar.

Their first move was to rig the September 1963 election of delegates to the Regional Congress. By this means, the Ba'thist radicals won all eight seats in the Regional Command, plus the majority of the delegates to the Sixth National Congress which met in October. The radicals, however, still did not feel completely sure of themselves, partly because of differences within their own ranks. They decided to refrain from ousting the Aflaqists in order to retain Aflaq's legitimizing image. But as an indication of things to come, a resolution was introduced at the congress condemning those who had failed to seize power in Syria before 1958. Later on in the congress, only one-third of the nine Syrian and Iraq positions on the National Command went to moderates. Aflaq held one of these, but al-Bitar was defeated in his bid. Supporters of Aflaq held four more seats as representatives of smaller branches of the party.[13]

But the Sixth National Congress of October, 1963 was concerned with more than a power play by the radicals. It was faced with devising an answer to a remark of Nasir's made during the Cairo Unity Talks and contained in the minutes of those talks the Ba'th claimed were selectively edited in Cairo to make Aflaq and al-Bitar look ridiculous. Nasir was quoted as saying that he had seen no particular ideological contribution by the Ba'th in recent years and that the differences between him and the party were political and personal. The Congress decided to issue a report outlining the differences. This report, apparently written by Yasin al-Hafiz, a Marxist-oriented Ba'thist, gave Arab unity a backseat to class struggle. On the whole, it was replete with Marxist-Leninist terminology and concepts adapted to, and often warped by, traditional Ba'thist ideology.   It was too idealistic and radical for most delegates and underwent many modifications in the original text before finally being passed--after the delegates refused to approve the report's introduction, which was written by Aflaq himself.[14]

The most striking feature of the Congress, besides the introduction of new terminology, was its irrelevance to existing political conditions in Syria and Iraq, two countries plainly not ready for the radical socialism envisaged by the report.

Also very interesting was the further indication of things to come, evidenced by resolutions over land redistribution and condemnation of favoritism in aid to cities over rural areas and to certain provinces over others.   The bitterness expressed in these resolutions clearly .indicated the poor, rural background of the overwhelming majority of the radical delegates.   Yet, for all its interesting facets, the report never did answer satisfactorily the arguments raised by Nasir.[15]

After the Congress, the Military Committee worked at consolidating its position by promoting Salah al-Jadid to major-general and appointing him chief-of-staff on November 11.   Al-Bitar resigned the next day, and the Committee took advantage of this opportunity to install Amin al-Hafiz as premier and Muhammad Umran as his deputy. Still, the new regime was immediately jeopardized by the 18 November coup in Baghdad which ousted the Iraqi Ba'th.   The new Iraqi leader was Abd al-Salam Arif, who was on very good terms with Nasir; thus Syria was once more isolated from its eastern neighbor.   The Baghdad coup also deepened the rift between the moderate and the radical wings of the Ba'th, the former blaming the loss of Iraq on the radicalism of the Iraq Ba'thi regime and the latter, supported by the Iraqis who managed to get to Damascus, on there

being insufficient socialism in Iraq.   The radicals
therefore claimed that in order to prevent the
same thing from happening in Syria the party
must undertake an immediate and radical transformation (inqilab) of Syrian society.[16]   More
important in terms of the Ba'th party within the
wider context of Arab politics was the downfall of
the Iraq Ba'thist party in 1963 which all but
destroyed the idea that the Ba'th Party could
become a power in pan-Arab politics and could
rival Nasir for leadership in the Middle East.[17]
In spite of this, Syria and Iraq continued their
vehement rhetoric against Egypt.

Nasir reasserted his leadership by calling for
a pan-Arab conference to meet in Cairo in January 1964 for the purpose of discussing what
action the Arab states should take over the
Israeli plan to divert water from the Jordan River
for its own use.   The Syrian delegation to this
conference was headed by Amin al-Hafiz who
called for war; he was very quickly put in his
place by the other delegates who understood the
purpose of the meeting, i.e., to put on a militant
and united face, but to do nothing concrete what-
soever.[18]

When al-Hafiz returned to Syria, the radicals
flexed their muscles at a meeting of Ba'thist
branch leaders by publicly upbraiding al-Hafiz for
not pressing for war.   The next day, 24 January, the radicals succeeded in getting al-Bitar
expelled from the party because of his signing
the resolution supporting secession from the
UAR.[19]

But the radicals were really not as strong as
these actions seemed to indicate.   By the end of
January 1964 they were faced with the potential
opposition of both the Military Committee and the
Aflaqists, who, despite their differences, were
ready to cooperate against the ultra-leftists whose

actions had led to public discontent with the party and had aroused the ire of the not inconsiderable numbers of conservatives and religiously-oriented Syrians. In early February this odd coalition expelled the ultra-leftists by increasing the number of delegates to the Regional Congress and packing in enough of their supporters to vote the radicals out.[20]

A new Regional Command was set up after the ouster of the radicals with eight civilian and seven military members. But since most of the civilian members were supporters of the Military Committee, Aflaq found his faction dominated by his recent comrades-in-politics who were only slightly less leftist than the radicals they had just expelled from the party.[21]

Aflaq called another National Congress in Cairo--an action which could supposedly be done only by the National Command - in which his supporters were the majority--in a ploy to get rid of the ultra-radicals on the pan-Arab bandwagon as had been done in Syria. To this end he filled new positions in regular and questionable branches--there were five representatives from the Yugoslavian branch of the party-with his supporters. The Congress then predictably elected a new National Command expelling or suspending the pan-Arab ultra-leftists as Aflaq had planned.[22]

Such events as the Cairo conference and the shenanigans in the party's congresses only served to intensify the Ba'th's difficulties in Syria and with the other Arab states.[23] On the Syrian level, public hostility was directed toward what were perceived as the atheistic, non-Muslim and heterodox Muslim aspects of the party and its members. From early February through mid-May in 1964, there was constant tension between the Ba'th and the conservatives, mostly Sunnis; this

tension often broke out into violent riots, pro-
voking in turn violent reaction from the Ba'thist-
controlled army. Many imams preached their
Friday sermons while dressed in shrouds, the
traditional attire worn when calling Muslims to a
holy war. In Hama, where much of the anti-
government reaction was taking place, the army
had to resort to the shelling of the Sultan Mosque
to quell disturbances. This action killed dozens
of protestors. Such harsh reaction kept the
unrest from spreading and the tensions slowly
died down.[24]

These events sharpened the differences between the Syrian and Iraqi Ba'th between which
mutual recriminations had reached a peak during
March-November, 1963. This period marked an
escalation in the acrimony and bombast between
the two Ba'thist branches and dealt with the
question of whether Syria or Iraq was the genuine leader of the National Command and of the
Ba'th. In Iraq many of the Syrian emigres began
to serve the Iraqi government's ideological
purposes. Living on handsome subsidies from the
Iraqi government, they became a source of irrita-
tion to non-Ba'thists, and in some cases, Iraqi
Ba'thist government officials. Although successful in extinguishing Nasirist activity in Syria, the
Ba'th had lost its moral strength and appeal in
the area of inter-Arab politics. From its
pre-eminent position in the movement for Arab
unity, the Ba'th Party, when in power, had
succeeded only in isolating Syria from its fellow
Arab states and itself from other unionist elements in those countries. Its actions made it
difficult to see very much difference between the
NCRC's 'enlightened' rule and the despotism of
men like Shishakli, whom the party had opposed
on democratic grounds. Then, too, the party
was quite clearly under the domination of the

military after it had spent many years decrying and opposing military rule.[25]

In an attempt to soften some of the domestic criticism, the Ba'th and al-Bitar, who was reinstated to membership after the ousting of the ultra-leftists, formed another cabinet on 9 May. Four days later the Presidency Council a new organization, vested with executive powers, was established. It consisted of five members, led by al-Hafiz who was promoted to major-general for the occasion. The other members were al-Bitar, Umran, the radical Minister of the Interior, Nur ad-Din al-Atasi, and the Druze leader, Mansur al-Atrash.[26]

This new arrangement helped soften or repudiate some of the more radical statements made by the ultra-left wing Ba'thists and became effective in diffusing somewhat the internal unrest. Thus by late June, the Military Committee had decided it no longer needed al-Bitar or the National Command. The military then began molding the party more to its liking, which meant making it a tool to be used as the Committee saw fit.[27]

Aflaq, realized this and understood what it meant for the future. He left Syria in an effort to put pressure on the Committee. Al-Bitar stayed behind to conduct a power struggle with the Military Committee and its civilian supporters, a battle which continued for three months. His was a losing battle, because the Regional Command, controlled by the Military Committee, had readmitted large numbers of the Regionalists (Qutriyyun) to party membership. These Regionalists sided with the Military Committee against the National Command, which was now being called Qawmiyyun, or pan-Arab nationalists. This cooperation gave the two groups nearly complete control of the Syrian party structure. To widen

their support among the people, the coalition set
up a 'dual organization' (al-tanzim al-muzdawaj),
under which members belonged not only to their
regional branch within Syria but also to more
restricted branches based on smaller localities,
professional or occupational groups, or other
bodies.   Although this 'dual organization' was
never effectively implemented, it showed the
intentions of the party, at least as it was
represented by the Regionalists and the Military
Committee, and what it felt needed to be done in
Syria.[28]

Salah al-Bitar did not agree with these
changes but he kept his post because of the
approach of the Second Arab Summit Conference
to be held between 5 and 18 September 1964 in
which Syria hoped to improve its relations with
other Arab States.[29]

After this conference, naturally, there were
no such compunctions.   Accordingly, on 25 September the Regional Command voted 'no confi-
dence' in al-Bitar's government which was then
forced to resign.   It was replaced by one headed
by Amin al-Hafiz, in which the regionalist militants were preponderant.   Al-Bitar and al-Atrash
thereupon resigned from the Presidency Council
to be replaced by Gen. Salah al-Jadid and Dr.
Yusuf al-Zu'ayyin, two radical Regionalists, a
sequence of events which completed the radicals'
takeover of the Council.[30]

Aflaq and al-Bitar counterattacked through
the National Command, hoping to take advantage
of a rivalry between al-Hafiz and Umran, the
latter of whom was in disfavor for recruiting
fellow Alawites for the military, for grumbling
about his unimportant post as deputy premier for
industrial affairs and for aspiring to be
chief-of-staff.   Al-Hafiz, with the help of al-Jadid
and Hafiz al-Asad, two Alawites, isolated Umran

politically; Umran turned to Aflaq and al-Bitar for
support.[31]

Aflaq returned to Damascus from self-exile in
Bonn and tried to set up a joint meeting of the
National and Syrian Regional Commands for the
purpose of embarrassing al-Hafiz.   Instead, the
Regional Command stripped Umran of his posts
and exiled him by making him ambassador to
Spain.   The National Command, still under Aflaq's
control, passed resolutions which declared the
Regional Command's action illegal and suspended
the Syrian Regional Command pending another
regional congress.   Much to their chagrin, the
members of the National Command discovered that
none of the regional secretaries in Syria supported this action.   The matter was academic,
anyway, since by that time the Military Committee
was in such complete control of the Syrian Ba'th
that the National Command of the Party would
have been powerless to oust them.[32]

These ineffectual maneuvers spurred al-Hafiz
and the Regional Command to take measures aimed
at strengthening their control.   These steps were
designed to neutralize the power of the upper
middle class and therefore were economic in
nature.   During the first four days of January
1965, the regime nationalized 114 business
concerns, from large companies to small work-
shops.   Agrarian reforms were speeded up to
increase support among the peasants and reduce
the holdings of the landlords.[33]

The middle class reacted by smuggling their
capital out of the country at an even faster rate
than they had before.   It is estimated that by the
end of 1964 capitalists had smuggled nearly one
billion Syrian pounds out of the country.   Reaction also came from the religious leaders who
began advocating civil disobedience.   Strikes were
dealt with quickly and severely; some participants

were sentenced to death as a deterent to others,
then quietly reprieved.   By now the Ba'th realized that it needed to control the ulama, men
learned in Islamic and Quranic studies, who form
the closest Muslim equivalent to Christian clergy.
The Ba'th tried to accomplish this by decreeing
on 28 January 1965 that the Presidency Council
had the power to appoint and dismiss members of
all religious hierarchies, whether Christian,
Muslim or heterodox.[34]

While trying to neutralize the ulama, the
Syrian Ba'th held elections to the upcoming
Regional Congress.   That factionalism was still
rampant within their midst was illustrated in
elections, held between January 10 and 24, in
which splits occurred along rural-urban, native-
outsider and regional lines.   The Aflaq-Bitar wing
tried to interfere in the elections, but with little
success.   The government sometimes tipped votes
in favor of one candidate or group.   Non Ba'thists even managed to meddle in some areas.   It
was obvious to the Regionalists and the Military
Committee that the party machinery needed over-
hauling.   As a result, they reduced the membership in the Regional Command of the Party to 11,
six of whom held no other political or military
posts so that they might devote all their time to
the Command.   This system was also adopted in
the regional branches within Syria.[35]

When the Regional Congress met, it com-
mended the Regional Command for its performance
and empowered it to nominate the members of the
Presidency Council and the premier.   The Congress also resolved that the regional secretary
would automatically be chairman of the Council.
Al-Hafiz, who was already premier, and his
supporters were in control of the Regional
Command.   They used their strength there to
appoint al-Hafiz regional secretary, thus making

him chairman of the Presidency Council. He now held the three[36] highest government positions simultaneously.

The Eighth National Congress was to follow the Regional Congress, but, in spite of their control of Syria, the members of the Syrian Regional Command were not happy about this prospect. For one thing, their moderate rivals, led by Aflaq, still constituted the majority bloc in the National Command of the Party. Secondly, there was an intense internal crisis burgeoning within the Syrian Ba'th, a crisis of which Aflaq was not yet aware. This crisis was within the military. When the Military Committee had found it necessary to come out into the open, it had tried to retain some measure of its secretiveness by establishing a Military Organization with 12 branches overseen by a central committee which was, in turn, supervised by the Military Committee itself. The problem and dissent arose because the top military and civilian posts went to selected members of the Military Committee, while the members of the Military Organization and certain founding members of the Military Committee got nothing. By not making any efforts to keep the 'have-nots' contented, the 'haves'--al-Hafiz, al-Jadid, and a few others--helped to widen the rift, a tendency intensified in late 1964 by the Hafiz-Umran rivalry. Consequently, the Regional Command tried to reach a reconciliation with the Aflaqists at the National Congress, held in April 1965, before the moderates found out about the schism. At the Congress, a committee composed of al-Hafiz, al-Jadid, Aflaq and Munif al-Razzaz, a Syrian-born Jordanian Ba'thist, drafted a report confirming the actions of the Regional Command in Syria in regard to the Military Committee and the Military Organization. But the report also reaffirmed the National

Command's supervisory power over the Regional
Command and transferred the power to nominate
the premier, the members of the Presidency
Council and the chief-of-staff from the Regional
Command alone to a joint session of both the
Regional and National Commands.[37]

Another important event had its genesis in
the Congress--Aflaq resigned from the position of
secretary-general of the Ba'th, a position he had
held since 1947; he was replaced by al-Razzaz.
Aflaq also refused to be considered for membership in the National Command, and when chosen
over his objections, refused to attend any of its
meetings for seven months. Whether he made
these moves as part of some pre-conceived plan
or not, Aflaq was unable to prevent al-Hafiz from
giving his support to Munif al-Razzaz.[38]

Soon thereafter, the split within the military
surfaced. Al-Razzaz was told that the Military
Committee no longer represented the Military
Organization and that al-Jadid had offered his
resignation as chief-of-staff after a vociferous
argument with one of the Committee's most vehement opponents, Major Salim Hatum, a Druze.
Al-Razzaz was then informed that al-Jadid had
retracted his offer to resign and would reconsider
it following a general military congress. This
congress, held at Kisweh in late April or early
May, was attended by three civilians, including
al-Razzaz, the first time the military had allowed
civilian observers at a high-level conference.[39]

Al-Razzaz has written that he was amazed by
the strong opposition to the Military Committee
displayed by delegates from the party's Military
branches who wanted the Committee deposed.
This objective was accomplished through a new
'Internal Regulation' which disestablished the
Military Committee and re-established the Officers'
Committee as a Ba'thist group. It should be

noted that during Syria's membership in the UAR and thereafter, the Officers' Committee, a long-established group, had been open to all officers for appointment regardless of political affiliation. The Officers' Committee was given complete jurisdiction over non-Ba'thist officers, but its actions concerning Ba'thists had to be approved by the Regional Command.[40] Despite this apparent setback, the members of the Military Committee suffered only minor limitations because they were able to occupy most of the top positions in both the Officers' Committee and the party's military bureau.[41]

Most important of the results of these congresses was the open eruption of the tension between al-Hafiz and al-Jadid. Completely different in background and disposition, the two also had different power bases. Al-Hafiz was generally supported by the Syrian populace, insofar as they supported anyone, while al-Jadid was backed by most of the officers whose support was essential. When one of these officers was transferred from director of intelligence to director of personnel, a reduction of prestige, al-Jadid resigned as chief-of-staff. Given his military backing this move amounted to a public threat to use violence. In an effort to avoid conflict, the Regional Command asked al-Jadid to meet with them and present his views; he accepted the invitation and, after denouncing Hafiz for misgovernment and economic incompetence, suggested the abolition of the Presidential Council.[42]

His proposal was taken up by a joint meeting of the Regional and National Commands of the Party in the last week of June, 1965. The delegates decided to keep the Presidency Council, but stipulated that its chairman--al-Hafiz--could not hold any other office. They then divided his duties as commander-in-chief between the minister of defense and the chief-of-staff, a position al-Jadid had resumed. Al-Hafiz refused to give up the premiership or any of his military power as long as al-Jadid was chief-of-staff. This time al-Jadid refused to resign. Exasperated by its inability to get either of the antagonists[43] to budge, the entire Regional Command resigned.

Such an action required a Regional Congress, and the National Command, in an effort to strengthen its position in Syria, decided to increase the number of members on the Regional Command from 11 to 16. But the plan backfired because of Aflaq's obstinate insistence that nine of the 16 members be from among his supporters. As a result of his unreasonableness, the other Ba'thists reacted unfavorably and chose 16 men known for their opposition to Aflaq.[44]

All of this infighting came at a time when the Ba'th's relations with Nasir's Egypt were again deteriorating, after having improved somewhat during late 1964 and early 1965. The problem was the perpetual inter-Arab question over how to deal with Israel. In this instance, Nasir was saying that each Arab state should defend itself and its anti-Israeli projects. Syria, which had had some equipment used in its Jordan River diversion project destroyed by Israeli air raids, advocated mutual help. Following a May conference in Cairo where the Syrian position was rejected, Damascus initiated a large-scale anti-Cairo propaganca campaign. Nasir replied in kind, and the vituperation continued until he threatened to boycott the Third Arab Summit Conference in Casablanca and all subsequent conferences. Knowing that the other Arab states wanted to continue the conferences and so would support Nasir to ensure his continued cooperation, the Ba'th had to back down. Otherwise,

Syria would become even more isolated from its fellow Arab states than previously, a position in which it often found itself. Therefore, the Syrian delegation to the Casablanca conference, led by al-Hafiz and al-Razzaz, acquiesced in all decisions made by the conference, including a resolution prohibiting any Arab nation from making propaganda attacks on any other Arab state.[45]

Al-Jadid and his faction seized this passivity as an opportunity to discredit al-Hafiz and the National Command, who had the uneviable task of explaining the Casablanca decision in light of their past invective against both Nasir and the Arab monarchs--an invective shared by the second echelon members of the Ba'th.[46] The Cairo and Casablanca Conferences discredited temporarily the leadership of al-Bitar, Aflaq and, even, al-Razzaz.[47]

On the home front the Syrian Regional Congress, which had met in March and April 1965, reconvened in June to approve a temporary program of action to be followed in Syria. This program had been formulated by the Regional Command, but it underwent some changes before its final approval, because the National Command had resumed its activity in Syria and demanded some voice in the program. The influence of Aflaq and al-Bitar was evident in several places and was especially heavy in the strongly anti-Marxist introduction. The program was approved by a joint session of the Regional and National Commands and was released on 22 July. Less than two weeks later, on 2 August, the National Command issued a program designed for the party in general. These programs were respectively known as the Temporary Program and the Party Program, of which the former was the most important insofar as Syria was concerned. On the whole, however, neither program actually added much new, but were mainly important in that they showed the Ba'th had effectively gained political and economic control of Syria and was acting to give a modus vivendi to those in the middle class who were willing to be reconciled to the regime.[48]

Throughout these Syrian-Egyptian and Regional Command-National Command scenarios, the Hafiz-Jadid struggle was continuing within the Syrian party branch and quickly became rather heated. Al-Jadid struck first by winning over four of al-Hafiz's supporters, including the minister of defense, General Hamad Ubayd, exploiting personal weaknesses and aspirations and the Ba'thist political system, which meant cementing political alliances on lines of confessional solidarity and distrust. Al-Jadid, who had castigated the disgraced Muhammad Umran for building an Alawi bloc of officers, himself inherited Umran's Alawi backing. In this regard it is interesting that al-Hafiz worked to rouse Sunni support for himself by making an issue out of sectarianism but the ploy failed, chiefly because Sunnis lacked the necessary cohesiveness. Most importantly, three of the four officers who left al-Hafiz for al-Jadid were not Alawite but Druze. Not traditionally allies, the Druze and Alawites found common ground when al-Hafiz raised the cry of sectarianism and over-representation of minorities in the officer corps.[49]

Al-Hafiz lost further support to al-Jadid when the former's actions made it seem that he was moving closer to the Aflaqists, thus 'betraying' the spirit of the 1963 coup. This came about because al-Hafiz was searching desperately for non-al-Jadid support within the party, while the Founding Fathers were seeking support within the military against al-Jadid.[50]

Such   maneuvers   created   two   broad   rival
factions   in   the   Syrian   Ba'th.   One   was   al-Jadid's
military   faction   and   its   civilian   supporters   in   the
Regional   Command   and   party   hierarchy;   the
second   was   the   very   fragile   coalition   between
al-Hafiz   and   the   Aflaqists.[51]

Power   shifted   to   the   al-Jadid   group   through
al-Jadid's   careful   manipulation   of   the   Regional
Command,   which   he   controlled   from   his   position   as
deputy-secretary,   and   through   defections   from
the   al-Hafiz   camp.   By   September   al-Jadid   was
able   to   withdraw   support   from   the   al-Hafiz   cabinet
after   al-Hafiz's   return   from   the   Casablanca   conference,   nominating   as   head   of   the   cabinet   one   of
his   supporters,   Yusuf   al-Zu'ayyin,   a   physician
who   had   served   as   a   volunteer   in   the   Algerian
revolution.[52]

Al-Zu'ayyin   formed   his   cabinet   on   September
23.   It   consisted   mostly   of   supporters   of   al-Jadid.
Dr.   Ibrahim   Makhus,   the   only   prominent   Alawi
civilian   in   the   Ba'th   and   another   veteran   of
Algeria,   became   deputy   premier   and   Minister   of
Foreign   Affairs.   A   Sunni,   Muhammad   Id   al-
Ashawi,   held   the   important   Ministry   of   the
Interior,   and   an   Isma'ili   officer,   Abd   al-Karim
al-Jundi,   headed   the   Ministry   of   Agrarian   Reform,
which   soon   would   become   an   important   post.[53]

In   an   effort   to   add   greater   control   over   the
military   to   considerable   civilian   power,   Jadid
transferred   'unreliable'   officers   to   less   sensitive
posts.   When   this   move   was   blocked   by   al-Hafiz,
who   still   wielded   significant   influence   in   the
army,   al-Jadid   resurrected   an   old   but   still   valid
law   which   gave   the   Minister   of   Defense--Ubayd,
who   now   supported   al-Jadid--the   power   to
transfer   officers.[54]

In   a   countermove   al-Hafiz   tried   to   reinstate
officer   friends   of   Akram   Hawrani,   who,   with   his
supporters,   was   charging   that   the   al-Zu'ayyin

government had a pro-Western oil policy because
it had signed a pipeline construction contract with
a British consortium. Hawrani claimed that the
terms of this contract were worse for Syria than
those with the Iraq Petroleum Company during the
French Mandate period.[55]

These charges generated wide discussion and
stirred up opposition within the Ba'th itself. To
rid itself of this pest, Hawrani (whose predictions
turned out to be only too correct), and to hurt
al-Hafiz's position at the same time, the government had Hawrani and his leading supporters
jailed on grounds of 'collusion with a foreign
power.' Al-Hafiz took the challenge and often
visited Hawrani in prison, and in December he
managed to get Hawrani released so that he could
go to Paris for medical treatment.[56]

Al-Hafiz then received help from a very
unlikely source when Umran, on leave from his
post in Spain, was reconciled with al-Hafiz--a
monumental task given their mutual animosity.
By this move, al-Hafiz hoped to draw away some
of al-Jadid's Alawi support.[57]

Unfortunately, the National Command was
split over the efficacy of this reconciliation.
Some members were opposed to conducting a
showdown policy with al-Jadid anyway, feeling
that they had neither enough political nor military
support to be successful. It was this group
which did not believe that the al-Hafiz-Umran
reconciliation could last.[58]

At this point al-Jadid made a tactical error
by having Colonel Mustafa Talas, who was stationed with the armored brigade in Homs, arrest
the brigade's commanding officer to ensure
al-Jadid's control of that brigade. Unfortunately
for al-Jadid, many officers were antagonized by
that action and switched their allegiance back to
the National Command. This loss of support gave

the al-Jadid-dominated Regional Command no choice but to acquiesce when the National Command of the Party voted on 19 December to dissolve the Regional Command and itself[59] assume all military and political power in Syria.

This decision was announced on 21 December, after which the Regional Command was replaced by a Supreme Party Command comprised of the National Command and al-Bitar and four of his Syrian supporters, thus giving the anti-Jadid faction a clear majority. Under the reorganization, civilian party members were included for the first time in the Military Bureau, and with the sole exception of service in the Ministry of Defense, officers could no longer hold military and government or party positions simultaneously. Party membership was also to be re-evaluated, since most branches were still loyal to the dissolved Regional Command.[60]

Al-Hafiz accepted these actions, although probably with reservations, even though they did signify the end to at least the political careers of the officers supporting al-Jadid, and quite possibly their military careers too, since Bitar was calling for another purge of the officers corps.[61]

For the time being al-Jadid and his supporters refrained from striking back, inspite of the fact that they had enough power to seize the government. Their opponents had not yet hit at the real bases of al-Jadid's power, so he and his supporters tried to avoid intra-party rivalries which had persisted throughout the history of the Ba'th regime in Syria. There was a tacit understanding that violent clashes likely to endanger the very existence of the regime should be avoided.[62] Additionally, an armed coup at that time would have had disastrous political consequences both domestically and internation-

ally.   So the al-Jadid faction instead undertook a
relatively peaceful program designed to embarrass
the new government.   Their first action was to
have al-Zu'ayyin, his cabinet and three of the
five members of the Presidency Council submit
their resignations, thereby creating a minor
constitutional crisis because only the full
Presidency Council, now reduced to two members,
could accept the resignation of the cabinet.   Six
days later the Council was restored to full[63]
membership and the resignations were accepted.

Al-Bitar was then asked to form another
government, but even before he accepted he ran
into difficulties, because the National Command of
the Party was not unanimous in approving al-
Bitar for the premiership.   For one thing, there
were still several supporters of al-Jadid on the
Command, and for another, some of Aflaq's supporters simply did not like al-Bitar for personal
reasons.[64]

Eventually, though, al-Bitar got down to the
business of forming the government.   One of his
first actions was to bring Umran back from
Madrid to be Minister of Defense--neither Aflaq
nor al-Bitar wanted al-Hafiz's group to be the
only military faction in the government.   Al-Hafiz
acquiesced in this move, but proposed that the
two joint offices of Defense Minister and Commander-in-Chief be separated with Umran holding
the former and himself the latter.   This was not
done, and Umran got both posts, alienating not
only al-Hafiz but neutral officers opposed to
Umran's sectarianism.[65]

Al-Bitar's first order of business, as announced in his speech of 4 January 1966 was to
end the isolation of the Ba'th both within Syria
and abroad, specifically by arranging a detente
with Nasir's Egypt.   To end this seemingly constant isolation, al-Bitar ordered the release of

political prisoners, including the supporters of
the Ba'th's old comrade-in-arms, Hawrani.   Al-
Bitar also asked those discontented with the state
of Syrian affairs to discuss problems with the
government, and he set up a committee to investi-
gate nationalized industries, causing rumors of
impending denationalization.   But al-Bitar made
one foolish mistake: he publicly announced that,
in accordance with an agreement reached with the
army before he had agreed to accept the premiership, he was intending to go through with the
transfers of officers considered hostile to the new
government.[66]

Al-Bitar was now in a dilemma.   He could
not transfer the officers he wanted without the
possibility of a coup.   On the other hand his
government would be seriously handicapped by
the presence of a hostile military faction:
members of which were in command of the army's
key posts and the Syrian party machinery.[67]

During the ensuing struggle for control of
the military and the party organization in Syria,
al-Jadid's faction had several imposing advantages.   They still controlled most of the party
machinery of the Regional Command, as well as
most of the Syrian sub-branches.   Well aware of
this, they resorted to a legal tactic, reminding
everyone concerned that the Eighth National
Congress had required the summoning of a
Regional Congress whenever a Regional Command
was dissolved.   As Aflaq and al-Bitar knew only
too well, such a Congress would support the
recently dissolved Regional Command.   To
counteract such a move Aflaq and al-Bitar
planned to purge the party's branches in Syria
and hinted at holding a Ninth National Congress
before holding elections to the Regional Congress,
a series of moves that would consume much
time.[68]

Itamar Rabinovich has remarked that, "Convinced of their own rightfulness and regarding the ousted Regional Command as a product of an illegal conspiracy against the party, 'Aflaq and Bitar were not so much bothered by moral scruples as they were troubled by the accumulating political effect that such accusations (of not having moral scruples) seemed to have."[69]

Their first move in the joint campaign, aimed to gain more control over the party and to neutralize the effect of these accusations was to prohibit temporarily any advancement of individuals into the higher ranks of membership, thereby keeping non-voting supporters of the old Regional Command disenfranchised. This tactic was supplemented by a proposed purge of several sub-branches in Syria (the Aleppo branch is the only one known to have been purged). The National Command also sent speakers to address meetings of members of 'second rank', but these speakers met hostile audiences, which were prepared in advance by the al-Jadid faction, with embarrassing questions.[70]

With the general failure of these measures, Aflaq and al-Bitar decided to implement a largely unsuccessful policy which they dubbed 'opening' (infitah), an apparently twofold plan to free the party from its exclusivity and to "emphasize its popular quality" by opening the Ba'th's ranks to mild unionists like the Socialist Union Movement.[71] Another move made about this time was the more successful restructuring of the NCRC by replacing 30 of its members and adding 39 additional members, thus bringing the total membership to 134. This move, and the limited success of "opening," gave the National Command of the Party the courage to call a Ninth National Congress and to prepare for the election of the Syrian delegates to that Congress.[72]

These two moves, coupled with the transfer of several of al-Jadid's supporters from sensitive posts near Damascus, would have seriously eroded al-Jadid's power base. It should have been obvious to the National Command that what it was doing would certainly provoke al-Jadid to attempt a coup, especially when Umran and al-Hafiz were caught up in their personal feud and thus were not likely to join forces to stop al-Jadid.[73]

Chapter VII

THE NEO-BA'TH: 1966-70

The coup was not long in coming. On 23
February 1966, al-Jadid's forces struck in Syria's
thirteenth and bloodiest coup in 17 years. With
General al-Hafiz al-Asad, one of the supporters of
Hafiz who had switched allegiances and joined
al-Jadid, controlling the air force, the outcome
was never in doubt. All the members of the
National Command who were unable to escape were
arrested, including al-Bitar, Umran and al-Hafiz,
the latter after putting up an hours-long fight at
his home, during which he was wounded. Al-Bitar
and Aflaq, the latter in hiding in Syria, and
several others were soon branded traitors and
"imperialist agents" and ejected from the party.
Later the two Founding Fathers were condemned to
death.[1]

On the day of the coup, the victorious
al-Jadid faction set up a Temporary Regional
Command, disbanded the NCRC and vested legislative
power in the president and the cabinet. Al-
Zu'ayyin again became premier; al-Asad was
rewarded for his help with the post of Defense
Minister; and Ahmad al-Suwaydani, a crony of
al-Jadid, became Chief-of-Staff. Two other
physician veterans of Algeria rose with their
comrade, al-Zu'ayyin. Drs. Nur ad-Din al-Atasi
and Ibrahim Makhus became President and Foreign
Minister, respectively.[2]

The coup and the events leading up to it
brought about several developments and changes in
Ba'thist and Syrian politics. On the level of
Ba'thist politics, the coup brought an end to the
often heavy-handed domination of the party by
Aflaq and al-Bitar. It is true that the two
founders managed to control some branches of the
Ba'th in other Arab states, but they were

overshadowed almost completely by the Syrian Ba'th after the coup. The coup also marked the beginning of a more distinctly Syrian, not to say Alawite character in the Syrian Ba'th, even though the new regime wanted to keep the Ba'th's pan-Arab character as an instrument of legitimacy and for interference in other Arab countries.[3]

For Syria, the power struggle showed vividly that the nature of politics in the country had changed: the sustained internecine struggle in which the Ba'th engaged without facing a serious threat by another political power to exploit the crisis was on index of a substantial change in Syrian politics.[4] The Ba'th was able to maintain its power during the crisis because most of the opposition parties, both on the right and the left, were exhausted by the years of useless struggle and almost constant repression. Also the Ba'thist officers had firm control of the army, enabling them to prevent any coup attempts when a situation became tense. Then, too, prior to the coup, the party had greatly broadened governmental control over public activity and expression and, through nationalizations and agrarian reforms, had obtained much of the power formerly held by individuals.[5]

The Neo-Ba'th also differed in several respects from the original Ba'th. The Neo-Ba'th began to take a harder line compared to the loftier, more abstract goals of the earlier Ba'th. This is particularly true with regard to revolutionary theory and tactics. Here it is important to note that the Neo-Ba'th depicted themselves as an opposition movement which emphasized, in its revolutionary guise, the practical side of Ba'th ideology. The Neo-Ba'th also interpreted differently the three pillars--unity, freedom, and socialism. The Neo-Ba'th concept of unity verged on the pan-Arabic idea; its mortal enemy was

Zionism. In fact one of the major differences
between the Ba'th (pre-1966) and Neo-Ba'th is
the degree that awareness of Israel and Zionism
played in their respective ideologies. While
present in pre-1966 ideologies, the apparent
danger from Israel became of paramount
importance afterwards. The role of Zionism as
conceived by the Ba'th and Neo-Ba'th has not
been studied sufficiently. It may have played a
more important role than has yet been recognized.

The Neo-Ba'th made a distinction between
personal freedom, not imminent of the horizon,
and collective freedom. The latter freedom was
the goal to be sought. The third principal,
Socialism, is for the Neo-Ba'th the way to
individual and collective personality. Neo-Ba'th
socialism was to bring into activity the Ba'th idea
of the 'ideal, i.e. abstract, utopian order.' The
Neo-Ba'thists sought to establish a concrete,
functioning social and economic system in place of
the Ba'th 'Ideal Order.' The Neo-Ba'th also
stressed education and through it greater
consciousness in the segment of the people that
would spur the revolution. It seems that by
'revolution' the Neo-Ba'th meant something
different from the inqilab of the former Ba'th
ideologues.

Werner Schmucker is of the opinion that the
chief ingredient of Neo-Ba'th success is that it
has made itself a part of the third world
revolution while maintaining its more important
local element which is adapted to Arab realities.
At the same time he stresses that Islamic religion
and its role in society present more of a dilemma
for the Neo-Ba'th which attempts to organize
itself along the lines of scientific socialism more
closely than the original Ba'th. Some of this
dilemma was diluted in the early seventies as the
stress on collectivism was lessened in Syria. The

Neo-Ba'thists in Syria have had to confront a war with Israel, the occupation of Lebanon and a sustained need for capital. The people possessing large amounts of capital were the main opponents of collectivism.[6]

Perhaps the most distinctive of the new regime's characteristics was its minority coloration--al-Jadid, al-Asad and Makhus were Alawis; Hamad Ubayd and Salim Hatum, two early members of the Military Committee, were Druzes; and Abd al-Karim al-Jundi, another early Committee member, was an Ismai'ili. At that time Alawis made up 11 percent of the Syrian population, Druzes three percent, and Ismai'lis less than one percent. In addition, all these minorities were predominantly rural, isolated economically, socially underprivileged, clannish in social structure and occult in religious tradition. They "could be expected...to display a populist agrarian-oriented radicalism, a resentment of the Sunni urban-based establishment, a penchant to rely on personal networks of relatives and friends, and something of a conspiratorial outlook. In addition, one might not expect so much pan-Arabist zeal from them as from the Sunnis."[7]

Syria's new leaders tried to better relations with Cairo in order to build up a Cairo-Damascus front against the so-called reactionary Arab states, especially Jordan. But instead of pleading for Nasir's good wishes, as the Ba'th had done on two previous occasions, the new regime tried to maneuver Nasir more to the left.[8]

Nasir responded cautiously. In June Makhus went to Cairo; soon after, Mahmud Riad, the Egyptian foreign minister and the pre-1958 ambassador to Damascus, flew to Syria. On 22 July, Nasir announced that he would not meet with 'reactionaries' at the Algiers summit meeting

scheduled for September. Finally these cautious
steps at rapproachement culminated in the 7
November signing of a mutual defense treaty,
through which Nasir probably hoped to get
advanced consultation and knowledge before the
fedayeen (Palestinian guerrillas) launched any
Syrian-sponsored attacks against Israel.[9]

On the international front Syria moved closer
to the Soviet Union which was at first apprehen-
sive that the left-wing al-Jadid faction would turn
to Communist China rather than to the USSR.
These fears on Moscow's part were allayed when
al-Zu'ayyin stated that Syria still considered the
USSR its best international ally. Soon thereafter, the Kremlin publicly gave its blessing to
the al-Jadid regime. But these developments
were still not entirely satisfying to Damascus,
since the Soviet Union would not officially
denounce Israel or supply SAM-2 (surface-to-air)
missiles to Syria. However, Syria did get help
from the Soviets in the form of funds for the
Euphrates Dam project--funds which the USSR
had declined to give in 1958 after the formation of
the UAR, on the grounds that the project was
'technically unfeasible.'[10]

Of more importance for the future was that
the Neo-Ba'th, as the Syrian Ba'th were now
officially dubbed, calling for an Algerian-type war
of liberation against Israel. This, of course, can
easily be attributed to the fact that al-Zu'ayyin,
Makhus and al-Atasi, as noted above, were
veterans of Algeria, and that Suwaydani had
studied Maoist guerrilla principles while he was
Syrian military attache in Peking.[11]

Consequently, the Neo-Ba'th strengthened
its ties with the Palestinian guerrillas, especially
with al-Fattah, led by Yasir Arafat. The Ba'th
had apparently first made contact with al-Fattah
in 1964, some two years prior to the ascent of the

Neo-Ba'th, when it realized that the then newly-created Palestine Liberation Organization (PLO) would be Egyptian-controlled.[12] Without casting doubts on the sincerity of the Neo-Ba'th toward the question of Palestine, it seems that the major incentive behind the renewal of these contacts was the Nasir-Ba'th contest for leadership in the Arab world.[13]

The al-Jadid regime was playing an intricate game in the leadership struggle with Nasir. It was trying to strengthen its ties with Egypt, while at the same time attempting to regain from Cairo some of Damascus's former pan-Arab leadership role and trying to goad Egypt into a tougher stance vis-a-vis Israel. The regime was also initiating al-Fattah attacks into Israel, usually from Jordanian territory, thus letting King Husayn bear the brunt of Israeli reprisal raids (even though Israel almost certainly knew that the instigator was really Syria). This gave Syria a means of hurting two enemies, Israel and Jordan, at the same time, without having to risk[14] too great a chance of getting hurt in return. By taking the lead in the fight against Israel the Neo-Ba'th had found, as one writer put it, 'the ideal stick' with which to beat Cairo, which would have to enter the fray, (although it was not ready to do so) and to grant recognition to the Damascus regime.[15]

But the al-Jadid regime miscalculated. Israel decided that the most effective counter measure was to launch verbal threats and actual attacks with the express purpose of toppling al-Jadid. King Husayn was independently working to achieve the same results. The Israeli attacks, the slackening of guerrilla forays early in 1967 (which brought charges that the government had given in to Egyptian and Soviet pressures to hold back the guerrillas), and radio broadcasts from

Jordan advocating the overthrow of the "godless'[16] Ba'th all encouraged opposition in Syria.

Religious right-wing protest flared danger-ously following an article in The People's Army (Jaysh al-Sha'ab), the army's official organ, on 25 April 1967 calling for rejection of "God, religion, feudalism, capitalism, colonialism, and all the values that prevailed under the old soci-ety." Widespread strikes and clashes broke out; the government broke the strikes and arrested the ringleaders; and then, to show that it was not "godless," sentenced the author of the article and the editor of the magazine to hard labor, although they were soon quietly released. To bolster its claims of Jordanian and Saudi Arabian complicity the regime expelled three Saudi diplomats.[17]

Meanwhile, Syria's complex maneuvers involving Egypt were having some results. Nasir, who had signed the mutual defense treaty for reasons stated above, found that his strategy had backfired. Instead of holding the Syrians in check for a while, the pact had been taken by the Neo-Ba'th as almost carte blanche to attack Israel. Nasir then had to cope with threats of Israeli reprisals. At the same time, he could not fail to support Syria, by which action he would lose much prestige in the Arab world.[18] Nasir's moves prior to the outbreak of war fall into five major categories after he decided in favor of maintaining his prestige in the Arab World. First, he got rid of the UN Emergency Force in Sinai. Second, he restored the blockade against Israeli shipping at Sharm al-Shaykh in defiance of the Saudis and Jordanians who said that he would not do so. Once having done this, Nasir intended to score a political victory over Israel which would enhance his position in the Arab world with an effect similar to that resulting from the Suez crisis.[19]

These actions by Nasir suited the Syrians very well, for, despite their bellicose stance against Israel, they were mainly concerned with driving Nasir into a tougher stance against Jordan and Saudi Arabia. This they had accomplished, but it had the unexpected and unforeseen result of leaving Husayn no choice but to sign a mutual defense pact with Egypt to decrease his isolation. The pact was signed on 30 May,[20] and, even though it was a direct result of their own scheming, it so angered the Syrians that they did not rush to help Egypt when Israel began its pre-emptive strikes on 5 June.[21] Even the pro-Zionist writers, Kimche and Bawly noted, "The Syrians, even at this late hour, were still more engrossed in their inter-Arab quarrels than in the war against Israel."[22] When Israel did turn its attention to Syria, it quickly destroyed the Syrian air force. The Syrian army fought bravely, but hopelessly, since it had no air support. The government itself contributed to the loss of Qunaytra (or Kuneitra) in the Golan Heights by announcing that the city had fallen, even though it had not been captured. This premature report, issued in an effort to strengthen Syria's position at the UN, panicked the soldiers in the Qunaytra area, who fled. Six hours later the Israelis walked in, virtually unopposed.[23]

In spite of the debacle of the Six-Day War, as the June 1967 war is generally called, the al-Jadid regime survived, "despite a thousand apparent reasons why it should fall at any moment."[24] One of the few historians to write of these events, Tabitha Petran, remarks however, that the defeat widened the void between the people and the government. Rumors that certain units of the army had been withdrawn from

fighting the mortal enemy enraged some people.
It was noted that, remarkably, Syria, which had
undergone 13 coups in 17 years was to suffer no
purges or even treason trials as a result of the
terrible losses it sustained.[25]
     Following 'the setback,' as the Syrians and
other Arab governments called the 1967 defeat,
Damascus called for constant guerrilla harassment
of Israel as well as an oil embargo and total
economic, political and cultural boycott of the
United States, Great Britain and West Germany.
But the regime still would not get together with
the 'reactionary' Arab states in order to present
a united front. As a consequence, Syria did not
receive the post-war largess for reconstruction
that Kuwait, Saudi Arabia and Libya paid to
Jordan and Egypt, although Kuwait did send
Syria some money, probably as an inducement to
reopen oil pipelines closed during the war.[26]
     Just as the regime refused to cooperate with
conservative Arab states, within Syria it refused
to cooperate with other progressive groups which
had proposed a national Progressive Front to
include Hawranists, Nasirists, the SUM and other
progressives, mostly former Ba'thists. The
regime's reply to the suggestion was widespread
repression and arrests; Hawrani himself barely
managed to escape to Lebanon.[27] Even though
the progressives formed the front in spite of
pressure from the government, the group lasted
only a short while before being fragmented by the
regime's practice of giving governmental posts to
some but not to others and by disagreement over
whether to help Iraq, where orthodox i.e.
Aflaqist Ba'thists seized the government again in
July 1968, in defiance of the Syrian Neo-Ba'th.[28]
This isolated the al-Jadid regime even more. It
was now cut off from the traditional Ba'thist,
from the Nasirists, the Socialists and the Middle

Classes of the cities.[29]

To remedy its isolation, the first step was the setting up of governmental mechanisms to plan and carry out the development program.   To this end the regime, which had entrusted al-Zu'ayyin with general supervision of the effort, set up a Higher Planning Council and a Planning Commission, a Central Statistical Bureau to provide necessary economic and social data and a Planning Institute to train planning experts and reduce reliance on non-Syrians.   In addition, the Ministry of Finance was reorganized and given more control over state finances.[30]

Under al-Zu'ayyin's leadership Syria made great strides, although in several areas the nation was hampered for lack of trained personnel.   And yet, as stressed in chapter four progress was being made.   By 1970 all land subject to redistribution had been appropriated, and by the end of 1971 85 percent had been reallocated to the peasant class, many of whom often rented the land right back to the original landlords.   Attempts to form peasant co-ops failed because of low educational and cultural levels and governmental inability to provide loans. Industrially, almost 90 percent of all large industries had been nationalized before the Ba'th took power, a process that the Neo-Ba'th continued.   Industrial development, however, was hamstrung for lack of trained technicians and administrators, unalleviated by the regime's habit of choosing them often only on the basis of loyalty to the party.   With Soviet help, the government began developing an oil industry, with the first exports shipped in July 1968. Unfortunately, the oil had a high sulphur content and did not bring high prices on the market.[31]

To improve medical services in rural areas, the Neo-Ba'th forced doctors to spend their first

two years after graduation in the countryside, a
law long on the books but generally unenforced
until then.   In addition, medical schools were
ordered to admit more students from rural areas,
even to lower admission standards if necessary.
In the sphere of education, all private schools
were put under state supervision, although
ownership remained unchanged, with the same
books and programs required in private as were
required in public schools.   Several religious
schools were closed for not complying with the
new measures.   Mathematics, science, practical
studies and technical education were emphasized
in the curriculum, and by the end of the 1969
school year, 68 percent of all secondary school
graduates had specialized in sciences.   The
regime also set up five higher technical schools,
including one in veterinary sciences and one in
electrical and petrochemical engineering.   In
addition, 23,000 Syrians studied abroad in 1969,
only 10 percent of whom went to communist
countries to study.   According to government
statistics, 90 percent of these students returned
to Syria.[32]

Despite the relatively encouraging development outlook, the Neo-Ba'th was undergoing a
process of factionalization, one of the characteristics it inherited from the old Ba'th.   This
factionalization went on mainly behind the scenes,
and its impetus was the war.   At its simplest, the
rivalry was a military-civilian split and a personal
power struggle between al-Jadid and al-Asad.   In
a larger sense it was a continuous conflict
between civilians and officers.[33]

Basically, the Neo-Ba'th at the beginning of
the June war was divided into four broad camps:
al-Jadid and his followers, principally Alawis
and/or officers; al-Asad's group; the Isma'ilis,
led by Khalid al-Jundi, Abd al-Karim al-Jundi and

Brigadier General Ahmad al-Mir, the commander of
the southern front; and a small group centered
around al-Suwaydani. After the war, the
Isma'ilis, generally considered more militant and
more pro-Chinese than other Ba'thists, soon lost
out. Al-Mir was removed as commander of the
Israeli front in what was widely assumed to be an
attempt to find a scapegoat.[34]
     Prior to the war, the military and political
Ba'th saw eye-to-eye on most issues, including
the issue of Palestine. But after the defeat some
of the military, particularly al-Asad, accused the
political leadership (which included al-Jadid and
some other officers) of ruining the army through
purges aimed at creating an army with the 'correct' ideology. The politicians retorted that the
army was incompetent, whereupon the military
demanded   rearmament   before   economic
development, as well as an end to political
interference in military matters, and total control
by the military over all paramilitary forces
fighting Israel, including the right to veto any
fedayeen (PLO) activities if necessary to lessen
Israeli retaliation.[35]
     Al-Jadid retaliated by beginning even more
extensive purges within the army and insisting on
the 'political purity' of the army and on the
rejection of any cooperation with the "reactionary" Arab states, even against Israel. He also
called for a popular war of liberation in Palestine
(which the Neo-Ba'th had been advocating for
several years), to which end he set up as-Sa'iqa
(The Lightning Bolt), a military organization
largely staffed by Palestinians.[36]
     More dissension had broken out in July 1968
following the Iraqi coup, heightened by the fact
that Amin al-Hafiz appeared in Baghdad soon
thereafter.   al-Asad proposed reconciliation
between the Neo-Ba'th and the old-line Ba'th, as

well as a broader program aimed at ending Syria's
isolation and strengthening the military. His plan
included the adoption of a more moderate line in
inter-Arab and international politics, plus the
resumption of participation in Arab summit
conferences.   Domestically,   it   called   for
supporting   the   Progressive   Front   and   the
readmittance of purged officers into the army.[37]

Such proposals were rejected by the Fourth
Regional Congress in September 1968, but, on the
whole, al-Asad had made some gains. Al-Zu'ayyin
and Makhus gave up their government posts, although they still remained members of the
Regional Command and al-Zu'ayyin still headed the
development effort. At the same time three of
al-Asad's   close   associates   were   given
newly-created   posts   as   deputy   defense
ministers.[38]

Asad eventually staged what Malcolm Kerr
has called a limited coup on 25 February of the
following year, seizing several newspapers and
the radio station and releasing political prisoners.
But because of his political weakness al-Asad had
to reach a compromise with the regime. This
compromise, ratified by the Emergency Regional
Congress of March 1969, provided that invective
against other Arab states would be softened, that
cooperation with other progressive groups in
Syria would be invited, and that a provisional
constitution would be promulgated. Elections to a
new Regional Command held at the Congress gave
representation to both the al-Jadid and the
al-Asad factions. Also, pursuant to al-Asad's
wishes, an Eastern Command made up of troops
from Syria, Egypt, Iraq and Jordan was set up
on the Israeli border.[39]

For the next year and a half al-Asad and
al-Jadid continued their power struggle, but on a
subdued basis.[40] However, the rivalry heated up

intensely following the September 1970 war
between the Jordanian monarchy and the
Palestinian guerrilla movement and the death of
Gamal abd al-Nasir. Syria sent an armored
column into Jordan to help guerrillas under siege
in the town of Irbid, near the Syrian-Jordanian
border; the Syrians claimed that the tanks in this
column were owned by the Palestine Liberation
Army (PLA). They were withdrawn after a few
days for reasons which are uncertain, but which
were probably a combination of Israeli and
American warnings and Soviet and Egyptian
advice.[41]

Rumors began circulating after the war, in
which the Palestinians were badly defeated, that
al-Asad had opposed intervention and had
withheld air support because of the international
implications. As the reports spread and the
Jadid-Asad dispute continued, the Ba'th held an
emergency session of the National Congress
(which by this time meant only delegates loyal to
the Neo-Ba'th and not to the old-line party), at
which al-Asad called for refraining from all
unnecessary acts of provocation which the enemy
(Israel) could use as a pretext to challenge the
Syrian Army and force upon it a battle which it
is in no position to undertake, and even less to
win today."[41] For his realism al-Asad was
roundly criticized as having a defeatist attitude,
and on November 12 the Congress passed a
resolution which complained that the Minister of
Defense had too much power and called for the
transfer of Asad and of General Talas, al-Asad's
right-hand man.[42]

Chapter VIII

Asad in Control: The Consolidation of the Regime,
1970-1975

In earlier chapters, we have noted how
minority groups such as the Alawites, Druzes and
Isma'ilis came to be so powerful in the Ba'th
party and in the military. But perhaps a few more
words are in order on this topic. Increasing
criticism was directed toward the al-Asad regime,
especially after 1975, for its 'sectarian,' i.e.,
Alawite bias. The al-Asad regime, whether justi-
fiably or not, began to be characterized by its
opponents as a sectarian regime. The contention
in this chapter is that this charge against the
al-Asad regime after 1975, weakened the regime's
ability to use Ba'thist ideology as a legitimizing
instrument for its main basis of power and, in
fact, after 1975 it became increasingly dependent
on Alawite regional and family connections to
maintain its hold on national power. Much of the
narrowing of the political and popular base of
al-Asad's regime and hence its vulnerability to
opposition, both internally and externally, was a
result of Syrian intervention in the Lebanese
civil war. As a result of its intervention in
Lebanon it was politically incapable of joining in
either the step-by-step diplomacy which the United
States, Israel and Egypt launched after the
October 1973 war or in the Camp David Accords of
1978.
As an example of external and Arab criticism
of the al-Asad regime, we can point out that the
emphasis on the 'Alawite' nature of the Syrian
regime became much greater after 1975 following
the Syrian intervention in Lebanon, this development also seems to have been encouraged by Israel,
to facilitate the negotiations for disengagement.
Some studies indicate that opposition to al-Asad

up to 1975 came from Alawites themselves,
especially from disgruntled pro-al-Jadid factions.
If, in fact, internal criticism came from Alawite
Jadidists, they had little to gain by criticizing
the alleged sectarianism of the Asad regime.
Following the disengagement agreements between
Israel and Egypt after the 1973 War, Radio Cairo,
largely because of differences between al-Asad
and al-Sadat over the disengagement diplomacy
with Israel, began to criticize the al-Asad regime.
On 26 April 1976, Radio Cairo stated that the
attempted coup against al-Asad, which had been
attempted a few months earlier, was "a mutiny of
the Ba'th party rank and file against the party
leadership for imposing the authority of the Alawi
religious community on the country." On 5 June
1976, Radio Cairo described Hafiz al-Asad's
regime as "the Syrian Ba'th Alawi Regime," and
on 25 March 1978, in retaliation for Asad's
criticism of his visit to Israel, al-Sadat branded
the Syrian Regime as..."firstly Alawi, secondly
Ba'thist and thirdly Syrian"... and to insinuate
that President Hafiz al-Asad had..."the intention
of setting up an Alawi state."[1]   Al-Sadat
continued to make such disparaging remarks. On
1 May 1979 he declared, "I was prepared to talk
on behalf of the Golan. But no. Let these dirty
Alawis speak for it. These people who have lost
all meaning of life. By God, let them face their
people in Syria and let them solve it. . . We all
know who the Alawis are in the eyes of the
Syrian people." King Faysal of Saudia Arabia,
before he was assassinated in 1975, had told
al-Sadat that "Hafiz al-Asad is Alawi and Ba'thist,
and one is more evil than the other."[2]   While one
has to interpret these remarks in the light of
al-Sadat's and Faysal's desire that Syria join in
the 'step-by-step' diplomacy, the comments are
also an indication of the Egyptian and Saudia

Arabian leaders' condescending attitude toward
the Alawites. Moreover a minority in power in
Syria only added to the Egyptian president's own
problem of dealing with the increasingly assertive
Christian Copts in his own country. But as we
have seen in previous chapters it was not
through the exploitation of sectarianism that the
Alawites gained and maintained power. Rather, it
was the party's socialistic, secularist and
pan-Syrian appeal that led the rural peoples to
support the Ba'th. Their support in turn led to
the over representation of non-urban classes in
the Ba'th party structure. In fact, it was the
preponderance of rural members in the various
party apparatuses which led al-Asad to take
measures aimed at broadening the non-Alawite
bases of power, at least, numerically, if not
actually within the important decision making
processes. It seemed for a while that al-Asad
was determined to return partially to the policy of
Aflaq and al-Bitar which "aimed to reach a
detente, and perhaps share power with the
party's urban rivals, dilute its radical program,
and push radical officer-politicians out of
politics."[3] It was just such a policy which had
appeared so threatening to the Ba'th's new elite
Ba'th's deriving from the villages under al-Jadid.
The history of the Ba'th, especially after 1963
was rent with ideological differences and
urban-rural cleavages: moderates tended to be
from the cities and hence were predominantly
Sunni; radicals, whether Alawite or Sunni, tended
to be from the rural or peripheral areas of the
country. As we have already described, through
a series of purges and other moves prior to and
during the al-Jadid regime, the power of the
Alawites in the military forces had been greatly
enhanced, so that Alawite influences in the armed
forces was a legacy of al-Jadid to al-Asad.

When Hafiz al-Asad assumed power in 1970, he was the only remaining member of the Military Committee formed during the days of the UAR. His assumption of power also indicated the increasing preponderance of power of the military wing of the Ba'th party while the civilian and regional apparatuses of the party, which included many supporters of Jadid, were reduced in power.

Al-Asad's first measures were to secure his regime and to avoid the very kind of coup d'etat that he had just staged. He assumed greater control of Ba'th political activities in the army and he attempted to ensure that his views rather than those of the al-Jadid faction would prevail. The reduction in power of the party also meant that attempts at mass mobilization and recruitment were to become less than during the Jadid regime.

Hafiz al-Asad assured officers through increasingly generous allowances of all kinds that they would be treated in a 'special' way: "Army cooperatives provide them with cost price articles and with duty free foreign imports which are unobtainable elsewhere in the country; interest free loans allow them to buy villas and to specu-late in very lucrative real estate; and they re-ceive generous salaries, free medical care, liber-al travel allowances, and miscellaneous other fringe benefits."[4] The military defense budget increased steadily during the first years of al-Asad's regime and by 1979 it had reached over one billion dollars, representing more than 25 percent of the budget, and supporting an army of some 230,000 men. As one scholar of Syria has observed, "If the armed forces do not stage a coup d'etat it will not be because their needs have been ignored."[5]

The al-Asad regime also sought to protect

itself against a coup by creating a special military
force of some 20,000 men reportedly all of Alawite
origin.   This force was to be solely dependent on
al-Asad and separate from the regular army.
Command of this so-called 'palace guard' or
al-Difa' al-Saraya was given to al-Asad's brother,
Rif'at al-Asad, whose own power increased
substantially.   In 1975, he was elected to the
powerful Syrian Regional Command of which his
brother was the Secretary-General.   It has been
suggested that Rif'at al-Asad was instrumental in
the replacement of Naji Jamil, one of the few
Sunnis in a position of top command and head of
the political department of the armed forces as
well as political security boss.[6]   In this fashion
the palace guard and its commander have been
clearly linked with the increased charges of
'sectarianism' against the al-Asad regime after
1975, especially since many of the top officers as
well as regular recruits come from al-Qardahah,
the home district of the al-Asad family.[7]   The
Difa' al-Saraya was outfitted with the best
equipment the Syrians could obtain.   In the years
since its creation it has apparently performed its
duty well and has been responsible for foiling
several assassination attempts against al-Asad and
members of his regime.   The 'two army' concept,
very ancient in its origin, is similar to that of
Saudi Arabia, where it too has proved effective.
But it has also been a center of the sectarian
charges leveled against the regime, especially
when Rif'at al-Asad himself and his top officers
became involved in the regime's increasingly
rampant corruption following its intervention in
Lebanon in 1976.   It should be noted that much
of the corruption also stemmed from Syrian
involvement in Lebanon.   Rif'at al-Asad was in
the vanguard of those who capitalized on the
possibilities of profit from the intervention.   But

despite all of the criticism of the 'imperial guards' and the greater opposition to the regime of his brother, and specifically from the Muslim Brotherhood after the massacre at the artillery school in Aleppo in June 1979, Rif'at al-Asad and his special force have maintained Hafiz al-Asad in power.[8] This supports the contention of many scholars of the Middle East and of Syria that in states such as Syria, Iraq, Saudia Arabia and Egypt, it has become increasingly difficult even to stage a coup d'etat because all of the security systems are in the hands of loyal adherents, whether ethnic, religious or regional--of the ruling regimes. Such situations account for the longevity of the regimes in the Middle East in recent decades, in spite of the fact that the area and the regimes are always characterized as unstable or that the entire region is in some kind of 'arc of instability.' Both Hafiz al-Asad and Saddam Husayn of Iraq have been effective rulers of their countries for a dozen years. Sadat of Egypt had been until his assassination in November, 1981, in power just as long. King Husayn of Jordan has ruled for over two decades. Thus short of a coup d'etat from within a ruler's own entourage or of a massive popular rebellion, such as that in Iran, it has been much more difficult of late to topple rulers. However, as we shall discuss later, a regime's narrow base can have quite negative effects on the body politic and on the ability of a government to institutionalize a broader base of power than that from which it first gained power, especially if power were gained through a coup. This seems to be the predicament into which Syria under al-Asad has fallen.

It is worthwhile of noting in this regard that during the first two years of al-Asad's rule most of the threats to his regime came from the supporters of Salah al-Jadid and other Alawites or minorities. Such a fact indicates both the effectiveness of his security measures and the weakness of his non-Alawite opposition. This situation was to exist throughout nearly the entire decade of the 1970's when a strong and broadly-based, and largely Sunni, opposition emerged. Furthermore, it is indicative that opposition became focused in sectarian religions garb. Until 1975-76, the[9] major challenges to al-Asad came from Alawites.

While al-Asad's first concerns were to secure his own regime and, indeed, his person via the mechanisms described above, he also attempted to broaden his support in the armed forces by appointing more Sunnis to top positions than had Salah al-Jadid. At the same time he made certain that real power remained in the hands of his loyal supporters, most of whom were Alawites. Naji Jamil and Mustafa Talas were appointed commanders of the air force and the army. Sunnis were appointed to top civilian posts as well. Abd al-Halim Khaddam became foreign minister, Abd al-Rahman al-Khilafawi held the prime ministership and a variety of other offices and Abdallah al-Ahmar, became assistant secretary-general of the Ba'th party.

Despite these appointments, opponents of the regime point out, particularly in the cases of Jamil and Talas, that these Sunni officers had no power because junior officers, invariably Alawite and supporters of the al-Asad regime, were the ones who were in effective command. It has been suggested that officers such as Talas and Jamil would exercise their power "only so long as they followed the President's policies."[10] Thus, the naming of Sunnis to top positions in the military as well as in non-military posts has, "been dis-

missed by opponents as a blatant attempt to dis-
guise the regime's narrow ethnic and geographic
base."[11]   In his   study   of   the   Syrian   Armed
Forces,   Professor   Drysdale   does   not   take   a
position regarding the Sunni's alleged lack of
power but he seems to agree with Nikolaos Van
Dam,   another   scholar   of   Syrian   political   and
military life, that Sunni officers do not form a
cohesive faction. Van Dam does contend that the
authority   of   high   ranking   Sunni   officers   is
short-circuited by second and third ranking
Alawite officers.[12]   On the other hand Raymond
Hinnebusch   thinks   that   such   statements   lack
credibility   in   lieu   of   an   "inside   study   of   the
Syrian army."   "If," asks Professor Hinnebusch,
"Alawite   officers   do,   in   their   second-rank
positions-as   division   and   brigade   commanders-
short-circuit the authority of the defense minister
and   chief-of-staff,   what   prevents   Sunni   officers
in   the   third-fourth-and   fifth-level   or   lower
commands   from   refusing   obedience   to   their
immediate Alawite superiors?"[13]   While I agree
with Hinnebusch that a detailed study of the
Syrian military must be made before final judgement can be made, it seems that there is some
credibility in Drysdale's and Van Dam's statements, for the Syrian army fought against Israel
in 1973 with little apparent disobedience to higher
command.   The Syrian soldiers, largely Sunni,
demonstrated   no   reluctance   to   fight   and   shell
Lebanese Sunnis, whether soldier or civilian.   It
would seem that obedience to command is stronger
in the lower echelons of the military.   Few coups
seem to come from the ranks of lieutenants and
captains, but rather from majors and colonels.
      Hafiz al-Asad sought to shore up his regime
through changes in the government as well as in
the   military   structure.   First,   he   had   himself

elected president in February 1971 and immediately organized a task force to write a draft constitution. The constitution, completed in 1973, grants great power to the presidency. The president determines and executes government policy, appoints and dismisses prime ministers and cabinets and promulgates laws. He can veto legislation[14] and has a determining voice in the judiciary. The cabinet is responsible and subordinate to the president. Its primary function, as in so many one-party, centralized, and authoritarian states, is largely to signal change in some party policy or direction of movement, while shuffling the cabinet and dismissing members also serves to pacify criticism, especially charges of corruption. This is not to say that cabinet members were mere figureheads. Many of them were chosen for their technical expertise in fields of finance and administration.

The centralization of the party as well as the government, when the two can be distinguished, also continued apace under al-Asad. The provincial Regional Command of the Party which al-Asad had appointed in the autumn of 1970 held elections in May 1971 and approved the policies implied in the 'corrective movement,' the name al-Asad had given his coup d'etat. Some new members, almost all Sunni, were added at the expense of other non-Alawite minorities. The National Congress also met in the summer of 1971, and al-Asad, not surprisingly, was elected its president. Al-Asad was reelected regional secretary-general and president of the National Congress in 1975 and again in 1980. In addition to these staged elections, al-Asad had become President of Syria in March 1971 in a pro-forma election.

In addition to the above measures, al-Asad made another attempt to broaden his political base by establishing a People's Council in February 1971. It held its first session in June 1973. He also created a National Progressive Front with the intention of including more of the leftist groups: Nasirirists, Socialists and Communists. The intention was that in the Nationalist Progressive Front these groups would be able to be more closely scrutinized by the al-Asad regime. The Progressive Front did, however, present a few problems. According to the Charter of the Federation of Arab Republics (FAR), signed on 17 April 1971 by Syria, Egypt and Libya (Sudan was to join later) members emulate the one-party structure of Egypt. This dictum was acceptable to the Ba'thists and the Nasirists, but the other progressive groups in Syria, e.g., the Communist Party, SUM (Socialist Union Movement), and the Arab Socialists, who claimed to be Hawranists, although Akram Hawrani, in exile in Beirut, did not believe in cooperating with the regime as his erstwhile followers were doing, insisted success- fully that the Progressive Front be an alliance of functioning parties rather than a conglomeration of officially dissolved organizations, as the FAR agreement would have required. Adding heat to the question was whether the communist party should be included at all, since the other three signatory states banned all communist activity in their countries. The question became even more heated when Egypt and Libya helped Sudanese strongman, General Ja'far Numayri to crush a pro-Communist coup in July 1971. Numayri retaliated by executing many communists and their sympathizers.[15]

Following the uproar in the Sudan, al-Asad rejected a demand by Libyan ruler, Mu'ammar al-Qaddafi, that he eject the communists from the Progressive Front and the government, and in August the Syrian Regional Command proposed to

the Eleventh National Congress a resolution which
would have glossed over the problem by having
the executed Sudanese designated as Qasimites,
'regionalists' and 'false progressives'. This tactic
not only solved the problem but the Syrian
Ba'thists were also able to make some ideological
points against their Ba'thist rivals in Baghdad.
In order to preserve some kind of credibility, the
National Congress rejected this ploy by a rather
substantial margin and passed another resolution
proclaiming the Progressive Front to be the only
workable political apparatus in Syria and
demanded its extension into all Arab states. But
the wafflings of the National Congress were
largely for propaganda purposes for al-Asad
hardly hoped for a viable Progressive Front in
his own Country.[16]

Up to 1975-76 then, Hafiz al-Asad was very
successful in consolidating his power, securing
the maintenance of his regime and broadening his
base of political power. While there have been
few studies of the Syrian political elite because of
lack of sufficient data, Alasdair Drysdale has
recently published a study which supports the
interpretation that al-Asad took measures, made
appointments, created institutions and implemented
policies during his first five or six years of rule
which in effect substantially broadened his base
of support.[17] Many of these measures have been
attributed to what some scholars have termed
Asad's 'pragmatism.' The implication follows that
the ideological content of his Ba'thism was weakened.[18] But in my opinion the statements
alleging pragmatism have been made largely to
indicate a contrast to the previous regime of
Salah al-Jadid. It would follow from this line of
interpretation that al-Jadid rather than al-Asad
more closely adhered to the original Ba'thist
principles. Such arguments also imply a greater

rigidity and inflexibility in Ba'thist ideas than exist.   One gathers the impression that if the regimes of al-Jadid and al-Asad were reversed, al-Jadid rather than al-Asad would be called 'pragmatic.'   Also the word pragmatic seems to be used almost synonymously with the term 'less ideological' hence to be pragmatic means to be less leftist-the implication being that leftists cannot be pragmatic.

Leaving aside the quibbling over terminology, what do the data from Drysdale's study indicate regarding the political base of the Ba'th party from 1966 to 1976?   Six years of this span cover a period under al-Asad's control. Comparing membership in the Regional Command of the Party with the geographic backgrounds for 44 out of 48 members, the data revealed that during the ten-year period only 5 members, representing 9.1 percent of the total membership, came from Damascus, which had 23.1 percent of the country's population according to the 1970 census.   But four peripheral provinces, Latakia, Dar'a, al-Suwayda and Dayr az-Zawr, contributed 75 percent of all members.   Two of those provinces, Latakia and Dar'a, had over fifty percent of the total membership in the Regional Command.   In the cabinet, Damascus and Aleppo with 44 percent of the total population occupied only 29.8 percent of the cabinet posts. Moreover, ministers from provinces such as Latakia served on an average eleven months longer in a given post than did their fellow Damascenes, indicating that they probably were more able to influence decision-making.   Also the key portfolios for defense, interior and foreign affairs fell to men from Latakia.   The paucity of representatives from Damascus and Aleppo is further revealed if one notes that only 16 percent of all Ba'th ministers originated from the key

cities during this period. The situation for the
Damascenes had been even more grim during the
regime of al-Jadid when they were apparently
unrepresented in the Regional Command. There
may well be a correlation between this data and
the fact that Damascus was a center of
disaffection under the al-Jadid regime.[19]

   The first cabinet after al-Asad's coup had
eight Damascenes, a 50 percent jump over the
previous cabinet. This increase was accomplished
by an increase in the size of the cabinet and by
a decrease in ministers from Dayr az-Zawr and
al-Suwayda. In other words, what al-Asad did
was to increase the power of Damascus vis-a-vis
the peripheral provinces which in turn enhanced
the position of Latakia.[20] Whether it was the
intention of al-Asad to form a new axis of power
between Latakia and Damascus is unclear, but the
indications of data up to 1976 suggest the
possibility.

   In the powerful Regional Command, Sunnis
still maintained 53.8 percent of all membership
and the Alawites 20.5 percent, but the Alawites
occupied the most influential positions along with
non-urban Sunnis. According to Drysdale, "prior
to 1970, the issue of Sunni political under-
representation posed a major threat to the regime.
In the R.C.S. (Regional Commands) formed in
1964 and 1968, for example, Sunnis accounted for
less than one-half of all members whose
affiliations were identified. Asad recognized the
dangers of this situation and matched his
conciliatory moves towards the cities with an
effort to improve Sunni access to political
decision-making positions. Hence, in the first
two commands formed after his coup, Sunnis
accounted for approximately three-quarters and
two-thirds respectively of all members. This
ethnic redistribution of power was not at the

expense of 'Alawis, who continued to form the
regime's inner core, but of the other
minorities."[21]   But not all Regional Command
members from Latakia were Alawites.   Most
notably, Abd-al-Halim Khaddam, a Sunni lawyer
from Baniyas, has been deputy prime minister and
minister of foreign affairs since 1970.[22]
    When al-Asad assumed power in 1970, he was
also riding the crest of a generational change in
age. He had the advantage of a youth boom. In
fact the Syrian Ba'th may have been the first
country in the Middle East to utilize successfully
the increasing proportion of young people in the
total population of the country.   This trend had
become very pronounced in all countries of the
Middle East where it is estimated that nearly 50
percent of the population was under sixteen years
of age.   The Ba'th Party in Iraq also appears to
have many youthful supporters, for, it must be
noted, Ba'th ideology had tremendous appeal to
young people.   In fact, Drysdale is of the opinion
that "The emergence of the more radical
Neo-Ba'th and the destruction of the Ba'th
veteran leadership between 1963 and 1966 was
associated with the ascendance within the party of
this younger cabinet."[23]   It could also be claimed
that the 'generational homogeneity' seemed to
lessen ideological, religious and ethnic
differences.   These factors seem to have added
further stabilization to al-Asad's regime after the
elimination of the more radical al-Jadid faction.
Yet, from 1966 to 1974 the average age of cabinet
ministers increased from 37 to 44, and it seems to
have been steadily advancing in the years since
1974.   While this tendency toward somewhat older
leadership is hardly cause for real concern at the
present, it will be a problem for the al-Asad
government if this trend continues.   On the other
hand the average increase of the age of ministers

has served may also give additional stability to the al-Asad regime.

Another factor whidh allowed al-Asad to consolidate his power during the first years of his rule and which contributed to the stability of his regime is the predominance of Syrian-educated persons among the elite. This shift reflects the more humble and rural origins of the Ba'th elite, especially after 1963, when comparisons are made with prior governments. While ideological, regional, and ethnic origins were the major considerations for Regional Command membership, it is nevertheless striking that from 1966 to 1976 not one holder of a degree foreign degree was a member of the Regional Command. Syria may be one of the few Third World countries in which the most powerful of the decision-making elite were educated within the country. Even in the cabinet, all but one of 15 persons who held the most important cabinet positions, were educated in Syria.[24] These factors may also be compared with the fact that 90 percent of the Regional Command members practiced just four professions–law, medicine, military, education (usually elementary or secondary)–and 52 percent of the cabinet ministers came from the same four professions. "Clearly many leading Ba'thists were professional colleagues, if not close friends, a decade before the revolution."[25] Also, a number of the Cabinet members must have been non-professional people. Hafiz al-Asad obviously had the advantage of utilizing many factors other than ideological, ethnic or religious during the decade of the 1970's, chief among these were a generational homogeneity, a similarity of occupations and an indigenously-educated elite.

The stability during the 1970's can also be attributed to the interlocking decision-making processes of the Ba'th Party, the defense establishment and the presidency.[26] The last position was protected by the 'imperial guards' under the command of the president's brother. All of these factors permitted al-Asad to prepare his government for war with Israel in conjunction with Egypt. They also permitted the Ba'th under al-Asad to extend its doctrine and strategies of development to those rural and petite bourgeoisie sectors which were underpinning his regime. Al-Asad's measures for land reform, land reclamation, irrigation projects and other undertakings continued apace during the turmoil and unsettled diplomatic situation after the 1973 war and amidst increasing differences with Egypt over how to conduct negotiations with Israel and the United States, while Israel occupied portions of its land, and when between 20 and 25 percent of Syria's budget was earmarked for defense.

Al-Asad thus seems to have had many things working in his favor during his first five years of rule, and he changed considerably the political, social and economic structure of Syria. Several scholars have pointed out that the mid-1970's and perhaps the year 1975 began to mark a decline in the vigor of the al-Asad regime. One of the main causes of the weakening of the al-Asad regime was the increased opposition centering on Syria's intervention in the Lebanese civil war. This burden, in turn, increased the vulnerability of the regime and resulted in the regime's greater reliance on Alawis, or, at least, the Alawites became more visible after the security forces were called upon to quell disturbances and to squash all opposition. In other words the ethnic composition of the government, especially as represented in the security forces which had previously operated behind the scenes were now more in the public eye. The average Syrian came to realize, as he had not before, the Alawite presence in the government. In fact the public prodded from external reports probably began to magnify the ethnic case and this in turn increased the charges against the government as being sectarian.

FOREIGN RELATIONS: 1970-75

Before turning to an account of the Lebanese civil war in the next chapter, an account of al-Asad's foreign policy during the years 1970 to 1975 is in order. As this chapter is being written in late summer 1981 there seems to be sufficient reason to conclude that, like al-Asad's domestic policy, the year 1975-76 seems pivotal for his foreign policy also.

Hafiz al-Asad's assumption of power in his coup of 13 November 1970 brought immediate benefits to Syria. Soon after the coup Colonel Mu'ammar al-Qaddafi, who had overthrown the Libyan monarchy on 1 September 1969, came to Damascus to give Syria $110 million and to promise $38 million more.[27] Al-Asad used this largesse to lower food prices, concurrently easing restrictions on foreign exchange, permitting more imports, allowing freer travel abroad, and increasing trade with Lebanon, Jordan and Iraq.[28]

December 1970 brought additional small but welcome changes. Al-Asad vistited Sudan, Egypt and Libya. Normal telephone connections with Amman were restored. Flights were allowed to be resumed by Saudi airlines, and al-Asad assured Lebanese Christian politicians that he respected

Lebanese independence. This pace continued into
January, when al-Asad released Syrians who had
been imprisoned on charges of aiding the regime
in Baghdad. Relations with Tunisia and Morocco,
two of Syria's old foes were normalized. The
American-owned Trans-Arabian Pipeline Company
was allowed to repair broken lines after it
promised higher payments to Syria. In February
al-Asad went to Moscow, where he dropped hints
that he might not fight UN Resolution 242 which
proposed Israeli withdrawal from lands occupied in
the June War of 1967 and Arab recognition of
Israel.[29]

One by-product of Hafiz al-Asad's fence-
mending was the December 1970 Tripoli Charter
States agreement, signed by Syria, Egypt, Libya
and Sudan, which proposed a federal union among
the four states. This gesture of Arab unity was
well-received in Syria and strengthened the
position of the al-Asad government there as well
as in the Middle East generally and allowed Anwar
al-Sadat to consolidate his power in Egypt. On
17 April 1971, the agreement was more-or-less
fulfilled by the formation of the Federation of
Arab Republics (FAR), which included Syria,
Egypt, and Libya. Sudan, in the midst of an
internal political crisis, did not join at this time,
but the way was left open for it to join later.
The FAR was a very loose union, so loose that
each of the member states was free to maintain its
own diplomatic relations, armed forces, and other
functions. Moreover, political party activity from
one nation to another was prohibited unless it was
part of the overall FAR program.[30] The last
stipulation endured for only a few months. In
the light of the subsequent development of bitter
relations between Libya and Egypt as al-Sadat
shifted his policies and priorities to Saudia
Arabia, it should be kept in mind that al-Sadat

used the FAR as a device to pacify leftist and pan-Arab proponents in Egypt while he consolidated further his own still precarious hold on power, especially against the supporters of Ali al-Sabri, his chief political rival.   Egypt had no intention of uniting with Libya except on its own terms.   Al-Asad certainly was aware of this, but the creation of the FAR also served as a necessary cover for preparations leading to the October 1973 war.

The creation of the FAR did cause some temporary difficulty to al-Asad when his new National Progressive Front included communists. This uneasiness moreover, has continued since 1972, even after al-Qaddafi and al-Sadat cooperated with General Ja'far Numayri of Sudan in crushing the communist attempt to topple his regime in July 1971.   But al-Asad's stance did not in any significant way affect his domestic policies.   This episode reveals al-Asad's ability until 1975-76 to direct his domestic and foreign policies along quite distinct lines.

Tension still existed between Jordan and Syria, in part because of events surrounding Jordan's suppression of the P.L.O. in September, 1970 (Black September), but after al-Asad took power Syrian officials initiated a more conciliatory policy towards Jordan.   When al-Asad was confirmed as President in a March 1971 election, King Husayn of Jordan sent a warmly congratulatory cable.   Husayn's brother, Crown Prince Hasan, visited Damascus on 18 March, but Syria still continued to express formal support for the fedayeen, a major cause of discord, until 7 April.   On 8 April, the General Talas, at the head of a Syrian military delegation, flew to Amman, to offer Husayn help in mediating between the government and the guerrillas. General Talas apparently managed to work out an agreement for the maintenance of peace,[31] although Husayn again cracked down on the Palestinians in July. Al-Asad felt obliged to close the border to Jordanian traffic and to bar air transportation to and from Jordan over Syrian territory. This boycott continued until December 1972 when al-Asad announced that just as he had closed the border for 'Arab reasons' so now he was reopening it for 'Arab Reasons.'[32] These beginnings led to a warm relationship between Syria and Jordan throughout the mid-1970's. Their relations cooled considerably in the late 1970's, however, as a result of the Lebanese civil war and religious opposition to Asad which was supported by Jordan and the outbreak of the Iranian revolution in 1978.

Another major component of al-Asad's foreign policy was to maintain the close relations with the Soviet Union, a continuation of a policy established during al-Jadid's rule. As a result, he received increased shipments of better quality weapons from the Soviets in spite of not signing a 'Treaty of Friendship' with Moscow as Iraq had done. The Soviets had requested such a move after Anwar al-Sadat, Nasir's successor, had expelled Soviet advisers and technicians from Egypt in 1972.

Meanwhile trouble was brewing for al-Asad on the pan-Arab front. He sent units of al-Sa'iqa and armored columns with PLA (Palestine Liberation Army) markings into Lebanon in April-May 1973 when the Lebanese army cracked down on Palestinian guerrillas in Lebanon, a scenario, at first, strongly reminiscent of the Jordanian-fedayeen-Syrian difficulties of 1970. This potentially dangerous squabble was resolved quickly in the face of threatened Israeli intervention. On the other hand, al-Asad tried to keep both al-Sa'iqa and the other Palestinian commando groups under tight rein in Syria because Israel viewed every guerrilla foray as grounds for massive and swift retaliation against neighboring Arab states--as Damascus had learned very forcibly after the murder of 11 Israeli athletes by guerrillas at the Munich Olympic Games in 1972.

After the massacre at Tel al-Zattar of the Palestinians by the Maronites, a truce came into affect between the forces in Lebanon.   President al-Sadat of Egypt then informed al-Asad that he intended to go to war against Israel if he could get support from Syria, Jordan and the oil-producing Arab states.   This initiative provided the impetus for a Syrian rapprochement with Jordan, heralded by General Talas' unexpected arrival in Amman on 29 August.   Two weeks later, on 12 September, al-Sadat, al-Asad and King Husayn met in Cairo, after which Syria resumed normal diplomatic relations with Jordan.[33]

Al-Sadat's oft-promised 'Year of Decision' came to fruition on 6 October with a joint Syrian-Egyptian offensive;   Jordan did not join the fray until several days later and then only half-heartedly.   Apparently, the Syrians, despite al-Asad's belligerent statements, aimed only at recovering a large part of the Golan Heights, which Israel had occupied in the 1967 war.   For the first four days, until 9 October, the Arabs clearly had the upper hand, restoring some of the self-respect they had lost in 1967 and before. They also inflicted heavy losses on Israel. Syria seized most of the Golan and threatened, this time more than verbally, to break into the valleys leading into Israel proper.   But less than a week later an Israeli counter-offensive had pushed the Syrians back past the 1967 armistice lines and had inflicted heavy losses on the Syrians, both in terms of men and materiel.   However, Israel did not try to take Damascus or to penetrate far enough into Syria to cause that country's downfall--which it probably could have done.[34]

Israel's reasons were probably largely political. They did, however, make a feint toward the Jabal al-Druze which implied they would welcome Druze collaboration. The feint toward the Jabal-al-Druze could also have been made for purely strategical reasons. Although Druze collaboration did not materialize, it is contended by Walter Laqueur that al-Asad probably did feel a bit threatened as the first senior officer executed by the Syrian government during the war was a Druze brigadier general.[35]

On 24 October al-Asad accepted UN Resolution 338, sponsored two days earlier by the Soviets and the United States, which called for an immediate ceasefire, negotiations and the implementation of UN Resolution 242 passed in 1967, calling for Israeli withdrawal from occupied lands. But he said he did so only on the understanding that Resolution 338 meant total Israeli withdrawal to its pre-June 1967 borders. Still, when the sections on the implementation of Resolution 242 and on negotiations are read together, the wording of Resolution 338 seems very ambiguous. Al-Asad admitted that resolution 338 had come as a surprise, but he said that al-Sadat had assured him that the withdrawal had been guaranteed by the Soviet Union, an assurance that proved fruitless in the coming years. Even Egypt's signing the Camp David Accords in September 1978 and the signing of a peace treaty with Israel on 26 March 1979 did not succeed in securing Israeli withdrawal from the Golan Heights from which she now guarded her water sources on the West Bank; indeed, as Israeli forces pulled back in stages from the Sinai peninsula, they extended their control over southern Lebanon. These three areas are of the most concern to Syria, and it was in Lebanon with the outbreak of civil war in 1975 that the major struggle between Syria and Israel was to take place in the late 1970's, and probably will continue to do so in the decade of the 1980's.

Chapter IX

The Moderation of Ideology,
The Evolution of Party and State: 1975-81

Many of the scholars concerned with Syria during the past decade and a half and who have written on Syria during the rule of Hafiz al-Asad such as John Devlin, Raymond Hinnebusch, Tabith Petran and Alasdair Drysdale have pointed to the increased pragmatism of the Asad government and the lessening of emphasis of the original principles of Ba'thism as conceived by the founders of the ideology and described in the first chapter. But as we have indicated earlier, much of Hafiz al-Asad's decreased emphasis on Ba'thism is a result of comparing his regime with that of the al-Jadid regime which lasted only four years. As a result of this comparison, the regime of Salah al-Jadid becomes the basis by which one judges how much more or less ideological the Asad regime is. But as was pointed out earlier, the policies which al-Jadid followed from 1966-70 were ones contested from 1963-66 and prior to 1963, and as far back as 1947, when the Ba'th party was not a major contender for power. By this logic al-Asad's regime would not be more pragmatic than the Ba'thist regimes or principles followed before 1966. But even this argument becomes unnecessarily semantic, because the policies pursued by al-Asad's government were and are not different from those visualized as being possible prior to 1966.

The policies Hafiz al-Asad utilized to secure his regime and to broaden his base of power are not more or less pragmatic than those of previous Ba'thist governments. The so-called pragmatism of al-Asad must not be considered as taking place at the expense of Ba'thism as an ideology, but as an evolution of the ideology reminiscent of previous changes. This evolution, it is true, did entail a moderation of certain Ba'thist principles in order to broaden the social base of the revolution, and in effect, to create a 'party' with a larger 'Syrian' base, if we include all of the social, religious and ethnic components of Syria as being 'Syrian.' Ideology cannot be expected to remain as powerful a force or to occupy as large a portion of policy-making when an 'ideological' party is simultaneously engaged in expanding its base of legitimacy. The main principles of Ba'th socialism and secularism remain pivotal to Ba'thism under al-Asad. The socialist appeal of Ba'thism under al-Asad has remained strong, especially in the rural areas of the country and up to 1975-6 quite strong in the smaller cities of the peripheral provinces also. The economy remains essentially socialist in spite of the infitah or opening to greater capitalistic economic measures and enticements which were introduced during the first few years of al-Asad's rule. In fact, the social policies of al-Asad's regime among the rural lower classes and petite bourgeoisie, which include many Sunnis, have been favorably accepted and have allowed the regime to withstand the largely middle and upper middle class religiously oriented opposition which began to emerge in the latter 1970's. There is evidence that the religious opposition has failed to gather significant support even from among the poorer urban-dwelling Sunnis.

Al-Asad has been successful in bridging many of the rural-urban cleavages which impeded the country-wide expansion of the Ba'th in the 1960's. It should be remembered that it was al-Asad's emphasis on secularism and his social policies which first rallied some of his supporters and potential supporters against him by the corruption which became rampant in the regime and in the party after 1975. From 1975 onwards it was corruption and a lack of party discipline which were the biggest obstacles to a further broadening of the regimse's composition by which means it could truly have become a party representing all of the various social groups in Syria and hence, for the first time in Syrian history, a truly 'Syrian' party. Since the mushrooming corruption and lack of party discipline were laid at the feet of the Alawis, this increased the polarization in the regime between and Sunni-led middle and upper classes and the Alawite-dominated upper military commands and the Regional Command of the Party. But it should be noted that the Alawites, some four decades after being a lowly minority which had been used by and had collaborated with the French, could sustain themselves in a struggle with the Sunnis for the dominant role in ruling Syria. This indicates the tremendous revolution which has taken place in Syrian society let alone the body politic: for the first time in the history of Syria a minority has participated in the sharing of power of the state and more importantly in the resources of the state. Indeed, it can be argued that under Hafiz al-Asad Syria for the first time became a state in the proper sense of that word. In no other Middle Eastern state are minorities so politically integrated into the state, if we take that word not in its cultural sense, but in the sense of proportionally sharing in the basic resources of the state as in Syria. This cannot be said of the Kurds in Iraq or Turkey or Iran, the Christians in Egypt since Nasir, the Sunnis and Bahais in Iran, and the Shi'i in Iraq, Turkey and Lebanon.

This is not to say that sectarianism or Alawiism was and is not a serious problem in

Syria in the late 1970's and early 1980's, but some of the disaffection has to do with corruption and even what one scholar has called, "over emancipation of formerly discriminated against Alawis."[2]

At a crucial point in the al-Asad regime's attempts to evolve a party with a state-wide legitimacy, further legitimization of the party was hindered by the decision of Syria to intervene in Lebanon in 1976. Preliminary studies indicate evidence of both Ba'th party and military support for al-Asad in regard to Syria's intervention in that country. In two perceptive articles written in 1978-9, A. E. Dawisha, a close observer of events in Syria, concluded that Syrian's intervention was based on four major perceptions: first, Syrian conviction that Israel is innately expansionist and desired, for security and water, to move to the Litani River; a move which would also increase Syria's strategic vulnerability; second, that Israel would use sectarian strife in Lebanon to reduce the effectiveness of Arab and Palestinian propaganda for a secular democratic Palestine; third, Syria's, and the Ba'th's, belief that Lebanon and Syria are integral parts of "Greater Syria" (Suriiya al-Kubra) and that the two countries were artificially created by France to serve its own imperial interests. The leadership of the Ba'th party and al-Asad himself have made many statements to support these ideas with, it might be added, the support of the great majority of Syrians. The Syrian government could not tolerate increased religious strife because of its own fragile religious balance, especially increased opposition from the Sunnis; fourth, the Ba'th, al-Asad and most Syrians perceived Syria as the birthplace of Arab Nationalism, and Syrians among its major purveyors.[3] In addition to these points, the

threat of intensified religious strife in Syria has
made the appeal of Arab Nationalism a more
durable political instrument than in other Arab
countries.[4]   Syria's involvement in Lebanon
increased stress on the trans-national aspects of
Ba'thism, especially in regard to Lebanon. Thus,
it could be argued that Syrian intervention in
Lebanon consolidated the decision-making process
among the Presidency, the Armed Forces and the
party itself. One should not conclude, however,
from this broad-based participation in the
decision-making process that Syria will be
successful in achieving its desired goals in
Lebanon, especially within a short period of time,
and an Israeli invasion would make the situation
more protracted. A. E. Dawisha has commented
that Syria's intervention in Lebanon was designed
to preserve the status quo. Intervention, it was
concluded, would be the best way to realize the
four strategic goals mentioned above.[5]   This
strategy, however, involved a misinterpretation
on the part of Syria of the primordial and
visceral hostilities which were involved in the
Lebanese war.   The hatred between the
conflicting groups became manifest as the war
progressed.[6]   It soon became clear that the
preservation of the status quo, even on a
reduced basis for the Maronites, required the
presence of 25,000 to 30,000 Syrian troops.
Since it seemed unlikely that Syria could maintain
this position indefinitely, she had two choices:
one was to eliminate the significance of the
Maronites; a second was to withdraw from
Lebanon altogether after establishing or
attempting to establish a pro-Syrian government
in power. An alternative to the above two
choices would be to re-establish its support of
the leftist-Palestinian alliance. The first choice
invited retaliation from Israel as did the third.

The second alternative would abrogate the original reasons for the intervention and could be taken only at the risk of great political loss and the probable fall of the al-Asad government. The Ba'th party, at least as it is presently constructed, would also be seriously jeopardized. The most attractive choice was to confront Israel with the hope that the super-powers would exercise constraint over Israel in view of their interest in the Israel-Egypt entente and the Soviet- American desire for some kind of accomodation in the Middle East despite an increase of tension between the two super powers after the Soviet invasion of Afghanistan in December 1979 and the tough rhetoric of the new administration of Ronald Reagan during its first months in office.

What has happened in the nearly three years since Professor Dawisha wrote his articles is a slight modification in the three choices to which Syria could avail herself. Syria did in fact choose to confront Israel, within the context of her other alternatives, in the hopes that the super powers would exercise restraint in concern for their interests. But after the devastating 1978 invasion by Israel into southern Lebanon which caused 5,000 Palestinian deaths and created an estimated 200,000 refugees, mostly poor Shi'i peasants who fled to the north, the Syrians began to opt more strongly for the alternative of consolidating their relations with the leftist-Palestinian alliance with whom they had renewed relations in late 1976. This in turn implied a reduction in the significance of the Maronites whom Syria had tolerated since the summer of 1976, despite their widely acknowledged Israeli military support and weapons supplies. Furthermore, Syria opted for this policy contrary to the belief that she would not

do so because of fear of Israeli retaliation. By
the fall of 1978 it would have been impossible for
Syria to withdraw from Lebanon without risking
the fall of the al-Asad government itself,
especially as the Sunni-led opposition intensified.
A Syrian withdrawal at this time would have
meant that the Ba'th party of Syria would have
been restructured would also be seriously
jeopardized. The most attractive choice was to
confront Israel with the hope that the
super-powers would exercise constraint over
Israel in view of their interest in the Israel-Egypt
entente and the Soviet- American desire for some
kind of accomodation in the Middle East despite an
increase of tension between the two super powers
after the Soviet invasion of Afghanistan in
December 1979 and the tough rhetoric of the new
administration of Ronald Reagan during its first
months in office.

What has happened in the nearly three years
since Professor Dawisha wrote his articles is a
slight modification in the three choices to which
Syria could avail herself. Syria did in fact
choose to confront Israel, within the context of
her other alternatives, in the hopes that the
super powers would exercise restraint in concern
for their interests. But after the devastating
1978 invasion by Israel into southern Lebanon
which created an estimated 200,000 refugees,
mostly poor Shi'i peasants who fled to the north,
the Syrians began to opt more strongly for the
alternative of consolidating their relations with
the leftist-Palestinian alliance with whom they had
renewed relations in late 1976. This in turn
implied a reduction in the significance of the
Maronites whom Syria had tolerated since the
summer of 1976, despite the by then widely
acknowledged Israeli support and supply of
weapons to them. Furthermore, Syria opted for

this policy contrary to the belief that she would
not do so because of fear of Israeli retaliation.
By the fall of 1978 it would have been impossible
for Syria to withdraw from Lebanon without
risking the fall of the al-Asad government itself,
especially as the Sunni led opposition intensified.
A Syrian withdrawal at this time would have
meant that the Ba'th party of Syria would have
been restructured drastically in the way it was
then constituted.

While approaching the reasons for Syria's
intervention from the perspective of the different
actors involved in the Lebanese civil war,
Professor Walid Khalidi is in basic agreement with
A. E. Dawisha regarding Syrian's policies in
Lebanon.[8] According to Khalidi, "It was
motivated by the desire to subjugate the Palestine
commandos in preparation for Syrian surrender at
the Geneva Peace Conference in the service of
Washington and Tel Aviv. Syria was also acting
in a Metternichean role on behalf of the
conservative Arab regimes who quaked at the idea
of the triumph of democracy and socialism in
Lebanon. The threat of partition by the Maronite
right was seen as a bluff that could and should
be called once and for all."[9] As a result, the
National Movement, the broad coalition of forces
representing the entire activist-Muslim,
Leftist-opposition saw the Syrian intervention as
"having snatched victory from their grasp under
the hypocritical cover of concern for the
prevention of the partition of the country by the
Maronites."[10]

There is other evidence that the attitude of
the Conservative Lebanese Front (CLF) during
the so-called sixth phase of the war from 1 June
to 22 September 1976, "was basically one of
acceptance,"[11] by Sulayman Franjiya, the
Maronite President of Lebanon and Pierre Jumayil,

the leader of the Phalangist Party (Hizb al-Kata'ib al-Lubnaniya). It seems that they believed the main objective of the Syrian intervention "was to curb the National Movement and to end the civil war by establishing law and order."[12] As indicated above, the Syrians probably never entertained the idea of eliminating the significance of the Maronites and neither did the Maronites, or leaders of the CLF perceive their intention as such. Elimination of the Maronites by the Syrians, even if it were achieved, would only have added to the suspicion among Middle Easterners that the war in Lebanon was instigated and encouraged by forces who had an interest in dividing Christian against Muslim in the Middle East, a policy which would seem to serve only the interests of Israel and in the late 1970's, and early 1980's, the United States. Syrian policy in Lebanon, however, was not static and it changed its support from the National Front and the Palestinians to the CLF as their foreign policy dictated. It is also possible that the Alawite regime in Damascus did not relish the idea of a Sunni state in Lebanon.

The hesitancy of Syria in pursuing what is perceived as its available options were the result, as Professor Khalidi has put it, of two nightmares: "that the Maronites would decide on partition, or that the National Movement would, with Palestinian help, rout the Maronites and establish a radical regime in Lebanon. There was little to choose between the two scenarios. The first promised to create a permanent thorn in Syria's side through the establishment of a new Maronite "Israel." It would encourage schism and centrifugal minority rights tendencies in Syria itself and throughout the region. The second, if successful, would create a beachhead against Syria for regimes hostile to it (e.g., Iraq), while at the same time serving as an alternative repository for Soviet favors. A radical Lebanese regime would by its very nature have imponderable results on the internal Syrian scene. It would be tempted to pursue a more belligerent policy against Israel. It could drag Syria into a war at a time and place not of its choosing. Either process--a Maronite movement towards partition, or a radical movement to topple the existing Lebanese regime--might at any moment provide Israel with a credible pretext for intervention, and so trigger a premature confrontation with it. Even the Sunni proclivities of a radical regime in Lebanon could prove to be threatening to al-Asad's regime. This threat became real, after 1976 when the Sunni-led 'Islamic opposition' began to challenge his regime. And even if the leftist forces succeeded in gaining control in a swift coup de main, the Israelis were bound to claim "compensation" by annexing southern Lebanon in anticipation of the[13] forthcoming militancy of the new radical regime.

Since the Lebanese civil war is such an important extension of the 'Arab-Israeli' conflict and of the United states' interests in the Middle east, mainly Persian Gulf oil, what was the U.S. attitude toward the Lebanese war and Syria's intervention? Again we must turn to the perceptive analysis of Professor Khalidi whom I quote in full, as to the political phases of the Lebanese war from Washington's perspective:

> The relaxation of Arab pressure for an overall Middle Eastern settlement during the remainder of the Ford administration; the breathing space won by Israel from harassment by the Palestinian commandos; the increased vulnerability of Asad making him more

amenable to Israeli demands in Lebanon and in the Middle East in general and his consequent automatic acquiescence in the renewal of the mandate of the United Nations Disengagement Observer Force installed after Golan I; the discomfiture of Moscow at internecine conflict between its Syrian and Palestinian allies; the tarnishing of the PLO's international image and its military domestication; the clobbering of the forces of the Lebanese Left; and last, but not least, the paradoxical strengthening of Egyptian President Sadat's position throughout this process.[14]

Nor should it be banished "into the realm of the unthinkable," states Professor Khalidi, 'that a deft push was given by some deft hand in Washington to events in Lebanon at some moment of partial stagnation."[15]

In the two years since the above assessment was given it remains remarkably perceptive, with the exception that in the summer of 1981 there was a war between Palestinians and Israel commencing in July with continued fighting into August. At the height of the fighting in July, Israel made a devastating bombing attack on Beirut in which some three hundred people were killed and another one thousand were injured. This bombing is evidence that the United States' desire to further domesticate the PLO, or to attempt to have Syria do it for them, was not carried out successfully as was perhaps anticipated. Much of this is due to Syria's perceived interest in reconsolidating her links with the PLO, if not as strongly with the PLO's ally, the Lebanese Left, which had been weakened seriously in the course of the Lebanese Civil War. This weakening was a move precipatated undoubtedly by one of the 'nightmares' of Syria in 1976 – the possible establishment of a new Maronite Israel, with all of its potential centrifugal repercussions in Syria. The possibility became more acute when Phalangist forces moved on the strategic city of Zahle in central Lebanon in April, 1981. This move, in turn, caused Syria to put air defense missiles on its border with Lebanon and the Biq'a valley which it controlled, and which is a strategic military route of invasion from the south.

The mission of American envoy Philip Habib in June and July 1981 was largely to restore the pre-Zahle balance between Israel and Syria. This was absolutely necessary if there were to be further negotiations regarding the conflict in the Middle East, whether along the lines of the Camp David Accords or whether through an inclusion of the PLO in some future talks. The possibility that Mr. Habib's mission and the guarantees which he procured from the respective parties, especially Syria, the PLO, and Israel would then be more comprehensive than a mere cease-fire agreement. However, this seems unlikely, and the policy followed from 1976 to 1981 will probably be continued, at the most, with some modification. It should be stressed, however, that there are increased pressures from the Arab world for some kind of settlement or, at least, that the United States should broach the idea of Palestinian participation. This is especially true after the Israeli destruction of the Osirak atomic reactor in Baghdad on 7 June 1981. This event, and this must be emphasized strongly, more than any other recent event, including the Palestinian question, shocked the moderate Arab regimes. They now had to ask the question which they had always avoided: just what were the American intentions? In trying to answer this question they were forced to come up with some unpleasant conclusions. Were the Americans going to acquiesce in a policy, carried out by its surrogate Israel, to keep the Arabs, whether it be Iraq or Saudia Arabia, from influencing policy in the Persian Gulf? The attack on the nuclear reactor was after all aimed at the very states which are not confrontational states with Israel--Iraq and Saudia Arabia. Furthermore, Saudia Arabia was a self-proclaimed friend of the United States. Arab states, whether radical or moderate, adjudged rightfully that the Israeli attack on the Osirak reactor on 7 June was aimed at the entire Arab world and it demonstrated that the United States was determined to go to such lengths to protect its dominant position, militarily and otherwise, in the Persian Gulf area, and Israel its dominant position both technologically and militarily in the Eastern Meditteranean. The escalation of hostilities in Lebanon to the level of all out war in July 1981, a month or so after the Baghdad raid, and the attack on the nuclear reactor must be considered the results of different policies. In short, the Israeli attack on the Baghdad nuclear facilities was to eliminate any possibility of contention by means of the nuclear lever from Iraq, and hence the Arabs, to be in a position to influence policy in the Persian Gulf for the next decade or so. The Israeli's also did not want the Arab i.e. Iraqi nuclear leverage over any expansion or annexation plans that the Israelis wanted to undertake in the West Bank, Southern Lebanon, or the Gulf during the 1980's. Since Israel did the deed, however, possibly with the knowledge of the United States and perhaps her assistance, she probably did expect United States acquiescence in her demands for

'compensation' on the West Bank and in Lebanon.
These perceived policies increased further Syria's
support for the PLO.

However much diplomatic activity swirled
around the above events, and these extremely
important consequences for nuclear warfare, it
seems unlikely that the basic policy interests of
the United States and, indeed, of Syria and
Israel, did change.   That is, that the Syrian-
Israeli-American tacit agreement, or as one
observer put it,menage-a-trois, which was put
into effect in 1976 with the Syrian intervention in
Lebanon had continued throughout 1981 and it
seems, despite increasing disgruntlement in the
Arab world, will continue, at least, for the next
few years.   What has, in effect resulted in
Lebanon is that Israel and Syria have gained
spheres of influence: Israel in the southern
enclave guarded by Major Sa'd Haddad and a
close alliance with the Phalangists, and Syria in
the eastern and central portions of the country.
Israel also has command of airspace over Lebanon.
Israeli command of the skies was only
intermittently contested by Syria in 1979 and in
1981.   Even after deploying air defense missiles
in the Biq'a valley in April 1981, the Syrian Air
Force did not contest the Israeli Air Force.
During the Israeli-palestinian hostilities of July
1981, the Israeli planes, American F-16s and
F-15s, met no opposition from Syrian aircraft.

One recent observer of the interpretation of
United States policy since 1976 has concluded that
"since 1976...it has actively sought to create and
perpetrate a state of 'controlled tension' in
Lebanon in order to distract Arab opposition to
the Egyptian-Israeli peace process, and to its[16]
possible extention to Jordan."   He does
conclude that perhaps United States policymakers
have little room or incentive to devise a more

far-reaching approach.   But whether one takes a
charitable or cynical point of view regarding
United States policy, it seems to have aimed at
creating stabilized spheres of Syrian and Israeli
influence.   This was a policy which..."stemmed in
the first instance from Washington's commitment to
the step-by-step effort to resolve the Arab-Israeli
conflict."[17]

But as this chapter is being written in late
summer 1981, there seems little likelihood of the
United States changing its step-by-step diplomacy
into a more comprehensive approach which would
meaningfully address the Palestinian question,
i.e., a sovereign Palestinian home on the West
Bank and in Gaza.   If this is not achieved, then
Syria's position vis-a-vis the Palestinians in
Lebanon will be very uncomfortable and the
results of this uneasiness would be felt
immediately in Syria and would put great pressure
on the al-Asad regime, a pressure it probably
could not sustain.   The possibility of the
Palestinians playing a role in the unseating of
Hafiz al-Asad in such a situation would be greater
than that of his Islamic opposition.   In the wake
of the events of the summer of 1981 the
Palestinians again rearmed, even purchasing
tanks.   But all of this leaves Syria in a dilemma.
She increased her support for the PLO as an
expression of her unhappiness with the isolation
in which she found herself as a result of
step-by-step diplomacy and especially the possible
reduction of what she perceived to be her sphere
of interest in the tacit Syrian- Israeli-American
agreement of 1976.   Also the al-Asad government
was beginning to be challenged by the Sunni
opposition led by the Ikwan al-Muslimin or Muslim
Brothers.   As a result, by the autumn of 1978
and early 1979, Syria had become even more of a
target of the diverse and conflicting groups in

Lebanon. No matter what she did, she would be criticized. Furthermore, her activities in Lebanon added fuel to the opposition and critics at home. Syrian involvement and success in Lebanon were connected intimately to the very survival of the al-Asad regime. Syria, more than anyone, wanted a settlement of the Palestinian question on terms which would not jeopardize the al-Asad government.

THE ISLAMIC OPPOSITION: 1975-81.

The second major problem which Hafiz al-Asad had to confront after 1975, in addition to Lebanon, was the opposition, religious in nature and led by the Ikwan al-Muslimin or Muslim Brothers which had its origins in Egypt in the 1930's and flourished until the 1950's when it was supressed by the Nasirist regime. It was during the 1930's that it established branches in Syria. However, the Muslim Brothers of the 1970's and 1980's in Syria are vastly different from the Muslim Brothers of the 1940's and 1950's. They are also different from the Islamic revival or resurgent Islamic groups in Iran led by the Ayatollah Khomeini which so captured the world's attention in the late 1970's after he was instrumental in toppling the Shah's government in January 1979.

But since the 'revival' or 'resurgence' of Islam has been such an important topic of concern for western nations and of Middle Eastern scholars, both western and indigenous, I think it important to state just how Syria's Islamic movement is similar or different from those in Libya, Iran, and Egypt, especially the latter two countries.[18]

Professor Ali Hillal Dessouki has recently

written that the so-called revival of Islam in the
Middle East is not simply a reaffirmation of
Muslims to their faith but that it reflects a
'society in crisis' situation which is characterized
by three phenomena: (1)   "Rapid urbanization
and an economic crisis that involves changes in
position of classes especially that of the lower
class; (2) loss of faith in western ideologies and
alienation; and (3) it reflects a problem of
legitimacy and of ineffective and/or corrupt
leadership.[19] According to this characterization
Professor Dessouki has arrived at four
propositions regarding Islamic revival in the
Middle East: First, that contemporary Islamic
resurgence should be understood in its
social-political rather than its religo-ethical or
ritualistic dimensions. Second, ruling elites in
Muslim countries may encourage Islamic groups as
a legitimizing device, a diversionary tactic from
other important issues and to discredit their
opponents, especially those of the left.
Generally, the more a political elite, in an Islamic
country, is lacking in legitimacy or is on the
defense, the more it will resort to Islamic
symbolism and religious legitimation. A third
proposition of Dessouki is that at the level of the
masses, Islam provides a frame of reference to
their collective consciousness, a symbol of
self-assertion and an identity rooted in one's own
history and tradition in opposition to foreign
penetration and domination. Lastly, Islamic
resurgence is most likely to occur in a situation
of economic stress and social-political alienation.
This occurs when recently urbanized sections of
the lower middle class are attracted to the call of
Islamic groups. It offers a defense mechanism to
protect their social status from further
deterioration and to keep the integrity of their
value system intact.[20]

When we scrutinize the three characteristics of a 'society-in-crisis' we see that number two, the loss of faith in western ideologies, is certainly no characteristic of the Ba'th and of the lower middle class constituency of the Ba'th in Syria. Of the four propositions which are a result of the social, economic, social-cultural and political characteristics of a 'society-in-crisis', Proposition Four is not even applicable. In fact, most of the explanations for the causes of Islamic revival which Professor Dessouki gives are more characteristic of Egypt and possibly Iran than Syria.

In spite of the different role of Islamic resurgence in Egypt and Syria, it would be profitable for us to pursue this matter in order to clarify just what is entailed in Islamic militancy. In this regard the result of two recent empirical studies of the Islamic movement in Egypt have just been published. They are important for they are the first such studies based on extensive interviews with Islamic militants.[21] These studies concluded that the five major Islamic movements in contemporary Egypt have grown principally out of the middle and lower sectors of the new middle class created during the Nasirist regime. Furthermore, their adherents are of recent rural background usually not more than one generation removed from the country and experiencing, for the first time, life in such a big city as Cairo where foreign influence and moral decadence of both western and eastern varieties are everyday facts of life. The people who fall into this category are exposed to the typical impersonalness of the city which is entirely new to them. Interestingly enough many of the students who support the militant Islamic groups are pursuing professionsl studies or scientific subjects. While all of the reasons for this are unclear, it may well be that these types of persons seek some moral order and rational explanation of the universe and their Islamic civilization. This conclusion may have substance if the students have not been subjected to elitist concepts by an urban educational system emphasizing the humanities and civil law. Seeking a better way of life, they have or are pursuing careers in technical and scientific areas. The sense of anomie and alienation of this group was increased by the national crisis of the Egyptian defeat by Israel in 1967, and the subsequent increase in the presence of foreigners--first Soviets and then Americans--and a deteriorating economic situation which fell most severely on those lower and middle sections of the new middle class who were striving to move up in society.[22] In addition, the more militant Islamic groups in Egypt were able to capitalize on the weakened position of the left who were daily categorized by the ruling elite as 'agents' of foreign powers. But Islamic militants could not be easily characterized as agents of the Soviet Union, America or Zionism-the three betes noires of the Islamic militants.

     In addition to these factors, the recruitment of members by the Islamic groups in Egypt was facilitated by the fact that most Egyptians, especially those of recent rural origin, were from a cultural milieu with strong communal attachments and in which a common attitude toward Islam prevailed. Lastly, the success of Ayatollah Khomeini in toppling the regime of the Shah gave a tremendous boost to all activist Islamic organizations throughout the Middle East, whatever their objectives and regardless of the social and political bases of their constituencies.[23] In short, Islamic organizations in whatever form, are still the most readily accessible solidarity groups for young Muslims.

When we turn to the Islamic movement in Syria, however, we see at once how greatly the structure of the Islamic opposition differs from those of Egypt or Iran.

The only detailed study of the Islamic movement in Syria has been written by Raymond Hinnebusch and he has come to the conclusion that the roots of Syria's Islamic movement and of its opposition to the Ba'thism of Hafiz al-Asad must be sought in four major factors.

First, the Islamic movement in Syria originally began as an indigenous reaction against the western-imported secular state. In Syria the movement seeks a reunion of political power and Islamic morality. This goal emerged more clearly after the traditional Sunni elite lost its power to the Ba'th after 1963. The movement received further adherents after the increased corruption of the al-Asad regime following 1976. These developments gave support to an appeal for an Islamic morality. Second, the Islamic opposition to the Ba'th and to the al-Asad regime is also an expression of a reaction by urban society against a rural-based regime to which it has lost most of its power. The historic ties of the 'ulama' or religious officials, to the urban merchant community has made it natural that Islam, interpreted to exclude 'socialism' would be used as a vehicle of ideological protest against the Ba'thist assault on urban interests. Hinnebusch further states..., "to a considerable extent, the cleavage between the Ba'th and political Islam represent a split between the city establishment and the village: Sunni as well as non-Sunni."[24]

Third, the Islamic opposition also expresses Sunni opposition to the disproportionate role played by members of the minority communities, especially the Alawites, in the Ba'th leadership.

Islamic   fundamentalism,   which   denies   the
legitimacy of rule of other than orthodox Muslims,
became a congenial ideological vehicle for it.

Lastly, according to Hinnebusch, the Islamic
movement   up   to   1981   has   been   chiefly   an
expression   of   urban-Sunni   opposition   to   rural
minority,   i.e.   Alawite   rule.   But   by   the
beginning of the late 1970's the opposition had
begun to become more of a 'ruled' against the
'rulers' than urban-Sunni against rural minority.
This clash opened the possibility that the Islamic
movement   could   perhaps   incorporate   those
elements of Syrian society which previously had
not been receptive to the 'call of Islam, notable
the Sunni segment of the modern middle class and
the   peasantry.   In   the   opinion   of   Hinnebusch,
"the   Islamic   movement   has   become   the   major
alternative tothe Ba'th, and the struggle between
these   two   forces...will   determine   the   future   of
Syrian political life."[25]

It is worthwhile noting at this point that the
Ba'th regime has recruited support from among
traditional rural Sunnis and even from among
pious ones.   This tendency increased during the
first years of Hafiz al-Asad's rule.   In a study
done among Sunni Muslim party recruits around
Damascus in the late mid-1970s, it was found that
19.7 percent of the recruits expected the Quran
and the Shari'a should have a large role in
legislation, 44.3 percent expected the Quran and
Shari'a to have some role, and 36.1 percent
expected them to have no role.[26]   This indicates
that the Ba'th policy under al-Asad remained
attractive to young rural Sunni youth even
though they had to subordinate their religious
feelings and non-secular values.   Concomitantly,
the strategy of the regime has been increasingly
to   break   away   from   open   and   aggressive
secularism, trying to blunt the issue, while its

enemies (the Islamic opposition) try to sharpen
and use the issue against it.[27]   It is significant
too that nationalism rather than secularism was
the major reason given for joining the party by
most recruits, 60.7% were from non-Ba'th families,
the sector from which the regime was most
ambitious to recruit.[28]   As a result of the above
study, Professor Hinnebusch concluded that the
Ba'thist recruitment policies have not
institutionalized a "regularized set of recruitment
rules and criteria capable of producing and
sustaining a homogenous elite and sub-elite
committed to a definite shared revolutionary vision
as a basis for decision-making and solidarity."[29]
In this regard it could be said that Ba'th
recruitment strategies under al-Asad have not
been as successful as such an objective would
require.   But if the major goal of the Ba'th was
the "consolidation of the Ba'thi political system
and the creation of a body of followers politically
loyal to the regime and to Ba'thist ideas in a
broad sense,"[30]   then it has been much more
successful.   It seems that this has been the goal
of the al-Asad government.   Its intervention in
Lebanon made it all the more necessary that it
follow this policy.

Hinnebusch concluded the above study with
the observation that,

> "Despite the fact that the party is seen by
> many Syrians as an Alouite preserve, and
> that Alouites are, for historical reasons,
> disproportionately represented in it, it is
> nevertheless true that the recruitment drive
> of the Asad regime has reached into all of
> Syria's religious communities and
> representatives of all of them can be found
> in the regime.   Despite the persistence of
> sectarian tensions and rivalries, the adhesion
> of the peripheral minority communites to the

center,   on   a   relatively   secular   ideological
basis,   will   probably   contribute   to   the   long
run   integration   of   the   larger   political
community."[31]

"It seems," he adds, "that class and urban-rural
differentations are being bridged, perhaps for the
first time in Syrian history. This may be a clue[32]
to the stability of the regime." During the
three years or so since this study was written it
has proven to be remarkably perceptive and this
is, in spite of the challenge, not noted in this
study, of the Islamic opposition which was to
increase in the late 1970's and early 1980's.

The big question which began to be asked,
especially after the Islamic-led revolution by
Ayatollah Khomeini in Iran, was and is, will the
Islamic opposition be able to topple al-Asad from
power? And if he is toppled from power will this
mean a fundamental change in the political
alignments of the Ba'th party? And even if
fundamental changes were to occur in the Ba'th
party, would the change in the prevailing social
structure of Syria be as drastic? Even if the
Sunnis were to come to power, what would either
of these two events mean for Syria?

The strongest support for the Islamic
movement in Syria comes from the traditional
urban quarters, i.e., merchants, artisans, 'Ulama
and notables and land owners who were
disenfranchised by the Ba'th. The merchants, as
in Iran, were alienated by the nationalization of
industry and of foreign and wholesale trade.
These restrictions on imports weakened greatly
the entire traditional distribution network of the
merchants. These changes, it whould be noted,
were a fundamental reason for the bazaaris or
merchants of Iran to give their support for the
overthrow of the Shah of Iran. Syria is vastly
different, however, from Iran and Egypt in other

respects.   For in Syria the Ba'th revolution took place in the countryside and the Islamic opposition, especially the Ikwan al-Muslimin, have not been able to penetrate effectively into the villages.   As of 1981 it seems that the Ikhwan have not established a bridgehead in the rural areas.   If the Islamic opposition remains largely urban, it will probably have little chance of successfully unseating Hafiz al-Asad unless Damascus itself becomes the center of rebellion. He is not likely to be unseated by rebellions in provincial cities, e.g.; Aleppo, Hama or Homs. Unlike in Iran where the Islamic opposition to the Shah was largely urban and allowed to grow, the al-Asad regime will and has used massive force in quelling rebellions and demonstrations in its large cities.   This point was demonstrated clearly as early June 1979 when some 50 to 60 cadets at the military academy in Aleppo were massacred by soldiers led by an officer recruited by the Muslim Brothers.[33]   On 23 June General Adnan Dabbagh, Syria's interior minister, reported that the massacre had been carried out by the Ikhwan.[34] The correspondent of the Christian Science Monitor reported that travelers arriving from Aleppo indicated that the fighting continued for several weeks.   Aleppo virtually sealed itself off from the rest of Syria until it was overrun by the imperial guard forces of Rif'at al-Asad.   The lesson of June 1979 was that rebellions in the cities would be repressed severely and that the army and special forces of Syria are increasingly well-prepared to squash such rebellions.

In spite of the severe repression in Aleppo in June 1979, there was continuing unrest in northern Syria from the fall of 1979 to the spring of 1981.   There was, in fact, a major offensive staged by the opposition, apparently largely Islamic, in Aleppo and Hama.   In the latter city, for over a decade and a half, the Ba'thist regime had been settling and giving land titles on the al-Ghab to Alawites from the Latakia region. The al-Ghab is the rich plain which surrounds Hama and which had been owned by the wealthy of Hama. This policy did not endear the Ba'thist regime to the notables of Hama. The fighting was severe and in Hama and Aleppo there were large scale demonstrations and areas of the two towns were able to shut out government forces. The lesson of the June 1979 massacre and of the spring uprising in 1980 was that there was substantial opposition to the al-Asad regime, especially in the northern cities. The regime, fearful of the example of Iran, began a massive counter-attack which continued through the fall of 1980. The measures the government took against the opposition were brutal, and marital law became the order of the day. The leaders of the Ikhwan were executed and membership in the Muslim Brothers became a capital offense. Al-Asad threatened and did arm his loyal civilian supporters from the various Ba'th party organizations against the opposition. His brother Rif'at threatened a blood bath.[35] Al-Asad seemed to aim much of his retaliation against that part of the opposition which emanated from the middle class. By the end of 1980, the government seemed to have effectively curtailed Muslim Brothers movement, the spearhead of the opposition to the regime. Without the Islamic cover provided the Brothers, the middle class and former land owners were unable to oppose the government in an effective way. However, well into 1981 the organ of the Muslim Brothers, al-Naseer, disseminated in western countries, continued to catalog the ongoing clashes between the mujahidin, or Islamic militants, and the al-Asad government.

In summary we can then cite several reasons for the weakness of the Islamic opposition in spite of its very real threat to the Hafiz al-Asad regime: first, the Ba'th appear more national-istic than the Islamic opposition; second, besides the Alawites, Syria's other minorities, Druzes, Ismai'ilis, Kurds, and Christians can only be suspicious of a government based on Islamic precepts; third, the Muslim Brothers have not been able to penetrate the villages of the army garrisons.   Moreover, many of the youth of the petite bourgeoisie, to whom Ba'thism still has a strong appeal seem committed to Ba'thism even as it has evolved under Hafiz al-Asad. Nevertheless, the events of the latter 1970s demonstrate dramatically the strains between a secular ideology, although more muted under al-Asad, and that of a society which still remains largely religious in its outlook.   In spite of great efforts expended by a host of Arab Nationalists and Ba'thist theoreticians to reconcile the disparities between them, the differences remain profound.   The riots at Hama and Homa in March and April of 1973 were caused by the publication of a constitution which did not state that Islam was the state religion.   A compromise amendment to the effect that 'Islam shall be the religion of the Head of State,' failed to quell the religious furor.   After temporary abatement it surfaced again in February 1976 when the Syrians turned against the Muslims (Lebanese and Palestinians) in Lebanon.   The situation was such that President al-Asad addressed the Nation on 12 April 1976 (in 1973 he had simply ordered the government to print a new Quran with his picture on the frontispiece; hence it was referred to as the 'Asad Quran') to stress the proper place of religion in politics.   It is interesting enough to quote in full:

> Every man can recall when we
> were students, we used to say:
> religion is for God and the
> homeland is for all. . . . the Moslem
> and the Christian in this country
> both believe that the relationship
> between citizens is first and fore-
> most the relationship of the home-
> land and Arabism. . . . The
> Moslem in this country takes an
> interest in the Arab citizen in
> Lebanon whether he is Christian or
> Moslem. . . Christianity and Islam
> issued from our land. This is not
> a burden for us or a problem for
> us; it is a source of pride for all
> our masses. These values emerged
> from our countries and our land. .
> . . We must be a nation worthy of
> these values, worthy of
> Christianity and Islam.[36]

I have no intention to discuss the history of
the Arab nations but a few points should be made
in reference to Syria within the context of
al-Asad's remarks. It was the Sunni Muslims of
Syria in the name of the political demands of Arab
Naionalism that sought the independence of Syria.
Paradoxically, they were not really interested in
the independence or the sovereignty of the Syrian
state.   In fact they wanted to disestablish the
state in favor of a larger Arab entity. Another
paradox is this philosophical or political
predilection contributed to the rise of the
Alawites who were more interested in the state
than in a larger entity. They desired a secular
state in which their rights and opportunities
would have some equivalency with the Sunni
majority.   In other words the concept of

'Syrianness' as expressed increasingly in the
1960's and 1970's was to be in the context of a
concept of state radically different from that of
the 1920's and 1930's.   But the Sunnis, the
dominate group during four hundred years of
Ottoman Sunni rule, believed. . .

> "it was their right to dominate the
> State and soon transformed the
> high hopes of the struggle for
> independence into a grievance.[37]
> A grievance, it might be added,
> sanctioned by divine law (Shari'a)
> which assigned dominance to the
> Sunnis.   If   nationalism   as
> described by Arab Nationalism
> theoreticians, e.g., Sati al-Husri,
> Abd al-Rahman al-Bazzaz, Michael
> Aflaq and Salah ad-Din al-Bitar,
> go hand in hand, then the Islamic
> part of that nationalism must be
> read Sunni."

Therefore, to the non-Muslims, Islam remains the
religion of a group of people who for centuries
dominated and hence felt superior to all other
Arabs.   Professor Kelidar mentions that Michael
Aflaq desired Arab nationalism to do for the
Arabs what Islam did for them in the name of
religious salvation.[38]   He remarks further on this
point that, "If this analogy is to be taken
seriously, then the orthodox Muslim must conclude
that if there is to be such a crusade, there is no
one who is better fitted and qualified to lead it
than themselves, and not the Christian Aflaq nor
the Alawi Asad."[39]
     While the Islamic opposition movement was
mounting its attacks against the Syrian
government from mid-1979 to late 1981, the Syrian

government continued its consolidation of power in Lebanon. In a series of meetings with Lebanese President Ilyas Sarkis, Syrian Foreign Minister, Abd al-Halim al-Khaddam, made four demands of the Lebanese: (1) a 50 percent share of revenues from Beirut's ports and airport; (2) an 'open' economy between Lebanon and Syria; (3) unification of the currencies; (4) a security pact which would permit a permanent Syrian presence in the Biq'a valley.[40] Even until mid-1979, Syria, in order to consolidate further its hold on its sphere of influence in Lebanon, did not directly confront the Maronites. One aspect of this accomodation seemed to be an increased role for the Maronite bourgeoisie and entrepreneurial class in a 'Greater Syrian' economy. This development appeared feasible as the Syrian commercial bourgeoisie regained some privileges from the economic liberalization which they had formerly lost. It would seem that the bureaucratic bourgeoisie, whose interest are closely linked to those of the commercial and entrepreneurial bourgeoisie, and substantially as well to those of foreign capital, would support a move in this direction. Muhammad Haydar, the vice-premier of the Syrian People's Council and in charge of economic affairs in Syria until 1976 remarked that under the al-Asad regime in the mid-1970's, "a new bourgeoisie has. . . developed in the shadow of the Ba'th party. Having been able to adapt itself to the new system we the Ba'th, established, it is richer and more widespread than the earlier. . . class."[41] If the external actors, Israel, the United States, the Soviet Union, and other Arab countries can be controlled, and the Arab countries could only aid such a development, Syria may well attempt a 'bourgeoisie' solution to the problem of Lebanon. That is, after pushing the Maronites into their traditional geographic areas and reducing their ability to exploit all of Lebanon for the particular benefit of the Maronites, they may invite the Lebanese Maronites and, indeed, elements of the Sunni bourgeoisie of Lebanon, along with the increased participation of the Syrian bourgeoisie, to participate in the economic arena of a Greater Syrian economy, with the exception of the southern enclave under Israeli control. There are many family, i.e. business connections, which would be used to implement such a program. This option would not augur well for the traditional economic principles and programs of Ba'thism, even as it became liberalized under al-Asad. But it seems such a policy could be carried out without denationalizing the major industries of the country. What would result from such a scenario is that Ba'thism would take on increasingly an even more traditional Syrian kind of character which would include more liberalization along capitalistic lines. As we noted earlier, there is further evidence of a kind of Syrianization occuring as a result of Syria's full scale movement into Lebanon. Oddly enough, if Israel were to expand into Lebanon, a similar kind of policy would likely follow, only Israel rather than Syria would be the dominant power. Part of the liberalization taking place is a result of the corruption which began to increase in the wake of Syrian involvement in Lebanon and which, in a slightly paradoxical fashion, was one of the reasons for the mobilization of opposition to Asad.

Before ending this essay a few remarks must be made about the possibilities of a Syrian-Iraq alliance based upon the principles of Ba'thism.[42] While the potential of such an alliance is great in terms of military power and economic and agricultural resources, the internal position of the two Ba'th parties and countries are too diverse to admit any viable or meaningful political cooperation. The hostility resulting from the split of the National Command of the Party in 1966 still rankles. The announcement by Iraq and Syria in the wake of the Israeli and Egyptian signing of the Camp David Accords and the creation of a 'Steadfastness Front' at the Baghdad summit in November, 1978 in opposition to the Camp David Accords, to unite their countries is evidence of the different aims and needs of the two countries. These conflicting goals emerge in spite of the fact that the two countries had reasons to bury the hatchet other than their opposition to Zionism and imperialism. Both countries wanted some protection in the last months of 1978 against the Islamic fundamentalists who were mounting what looked like an increasingly successful attack against the Shah of Iran. Iraq was fearful of the Islamic revolution spreading to its southern Shi'i population and al-Asad already was being confronted by an Islamic-oriented opposition. In addition al-Asad was anxious to cover his eastern flank while his forces were bogged down in Lebanon. Al-Asad was furthermore hopeful that Iraq would be generous with some of its petro dollars. Syria was in need of aid because of the high inflation which hit it after 1975, one of the results of her intervention into Lebanon. A union with Iraq in the winter of 1978 would perhaps also have speeded up the shipments of Soviet arms at a time when the Soviets had been dragging their heels. Iraq, in turn, thought that a union with Syria would give her a greater voice, or, at least, more manipulative room in Lebanon, if not in Syrian politics.[43]

The announcement of Syrian-Iraq 'unity' in November 1978, to no one's surprise, failed to

materialize, it had not been intended to do so.
Again in the aftermath of the Israeli bombing
attack on Iraq's nuclear reactor on 7 June 1981
there was discussion in the press about a [44]
potential unification between the two countries.
The Iraqis proposed increasing the flow of Iraqi
oil through the Syrian pipeline to the
Mediterranean from 100,000 to 500,000 barrels per
day, with 25 cents of every barrel shipped, going
to the Syrians. But the Syrians turned them
down. Undoubtedly the hostile Iraqi policy from
spring 1979 to 1981 played a role in Syria's
decision. During this period of time it was being
alleged that Iraq was involved in supporting some
of the oppositional groups to the, al-Asad regime.
These acts of Iraq also played a role in Syria's
support of the Iranian revolution in 1979 and
support for Iran when war broke out between
that country and Iraq in September 1980.

As we discussed above, the Israeli air attack
on the nuclear reactor in Baghdad was
undoubtedly one of the most severe psychological
blows which all Arabs have had to face since the
June defeat of 1967. The attack indicated clearly
that the policy of the United States in possible,
or, at least de facto collaboration with Israel
would allow no threat to its position in the
Persian Gulf. It also demonstrated emphatically
that Iraq is a Persian Gulf country and Syria is
an eastern Mediterranean country. Culturally,
administratively, agriculturally Iraq is simply a
more underdeveloped polity. This is reflected in
the reported differences between the Syrians who
fled to Iraq in the 1960's and their Iraqi hosts.
In addition to the fundamental historical
differences described above, Iraq's preoccupation
with its war wtih Iran and its attempts to
consolidate its power and position on the Persian
Gulf, will occupy its attention throughout the

1980's; just as Syria will be occupied with Lebanon and all that it entails. This does not rule out that from time to time the two countries will forge tactical alliances against their chief nemeses, Israel and the United States. In addition to the above, there are rising problems within the Iraqi Ba'th party itself. The chief problem stems from the fact that the leadership of the Iraqi Ba'th derives nearly entirely from the Tulfah family of Takrit. Practically all of the top leaders of the National, Regional and Military Commands are connected to this family in one way or the other. In some instances the Tulfah family of Takrit is joined by groups from Samarra, a town close to Takrit, and from Anah, a town on the Euphrates near the Syrian border. This geographical concentration is fully evident in the structure of the Regional Command of the Ba'th Party. Fifty-two percent of the seventy-two percent of the Regional Command originate from the northern cities, Takrit, Sammara and Anah and they also hold the top positions. This configuration of power and geography may also have a bearing on the subject of a potential Iraqi-Syrian alliance. Many of the Iraqi Ba'th members who come from Anah and Rawwah on the Syrian border have maintained close ties with the Arab Sunni Ba'thists in Syria--although not the Alawites. Since 1966, when several thousand Syrians, eventually including Aflaq himself, fled to Iraq they were important protaganists for the Iraqi regime in their differences with the Syrian branch of the party. While their power has diminished somewhat since that time, they are still a source of support for the regime and increasingly a target of criticism from the professional and, especially, the intelligentsia class who have chafed at Syrian airs of superiority over their Iraqi counterparts. The

hostilities between the refugees from Syria and
the Iraqis, especially university professors and
the intelligentsia, has been much more profound
than is usually realized.

There are other internal factors in Iraq
which militate against meaningful political union
with Syria. The increased emphasis on
personalism and the cult of personality so evident
at times in the politics of the Middle East, seems
to be occurring in Iraq under the leadership of
Saddam Husayn. Husayn's encouragement of the
cult of his own personality is compounded by
Takriti nepotism. The new and younger members
of the party who joined in the 1960's chafe at the
lack of advancement in return for their party
loyalty. Also the civilian section of the party has
not been as prominent in the decision-making
arena as in Syria. The military in Iraq retains
paramountcy and, until the war with Iran ends,
is bound to continue. The problem with the
Kurds and Shi'is will undoubtedly continue this
trend, unlike in Syria, where the civilian arm of
the party might serve an important role in the
incorporation of the Lebanese economy into the
Syrian economy.

The lack of support from the intelligentsia,
largely Sunni, is important in itself and
exacerbates the above problems. Criticism of
the regime has led to over 100-150 dismissals from
universities during 1978 and the first half of
1979. The opposition of the intelligentsia and the
professional classes on which the regime must
depend for rapid development, particularly in the
economic sphere, is ominous as the role which
they play is similar to that of their counterparts
in Iran. While Syria has many of the same
problems as Iraq, they are not as acute. In this
regard it must be kept in mind that Syrian
political and economic development historically was

much in advance of that in Iraq, in spite of dramatic gains by Iraq in the 1970s.

In August 1979 Iraq expelled the Syrian mission from Baghdad. In sum, Syria, because of its support for Iran, has played no role in the Iraqi diplomacy of 1980 which brought Iraq, Saudi Arabia, Jordan and the Gulf States into a closer relationship. The Iraqi-Iran war did, however, allow Syria to mop up the remnants of the Muslim Brothers with less interference than usual from Iraq, Jordan and Saudia Arabia. As a result of the war, Syria's and Jordan's strained relations also improved marginally in the 1981, if only because the Iran-Iraq war made Jordan less able to support of to offer sanctuary to the Brothers. When Syria moved troops to the borders of Jordan in the last months of 1980, it was largely to intimidate her into stopping the support of the Muslim Brotherhood and ending Jordan's alleged refuge of them. King Husayn was forced to back down and a few months later he announced his support for Iraq in its war against Iran. Syria continued to support Iran. All of these events allowed the al-Asad regime to regain its composure. As this chapter is being written it seems that a continuation of the Iraq-Iran war will aid Hafiz al-Asad in his forward policy against his 'Islamic' opposition. But a settlement of the Iran-Iraq War will undoubtedly once again raise the challenge of the 'Islamic opposition' to al-Asad's regime, and the opposition might well be supported more vigorously by Iraq, Jordan, Egypt and Saudi Arabia.

CONCLUSION

From an historical point of view the Ba'th revolution in Syria has brought about many fundamental and positive changes in Syria. During the thirty-four year period which this book spans, 1947 to 1981, revolutionary changes have occurred in the social structure of Syria. A major revolution has occurred in the relationships between rural areas and the urban centers in terms of political representation. Another completely unanticipated development has been the accession to power in the 1960's of the Alawites-a poor, rural, and non-Sunni group representing only 11 percent of the population. The Alawites' assumption of power is a remarkable example of how an ideology, coupled with military power in the hands of a minority and a profession of faith different from the traditional elites, can be used to develop the political structure and to create social change within a country. It should be pointed out, however, that this change was not a conscious strategy of development emanating from the ideology of Ba'thism itself. It is highly doubtful that the Ba'thist revolution from 1962 to 1975 in Syria would have been as successful as it has been if it had not been led by the Alawites. The bridging of the gap between the traditional Sunni-urban elite and the poor provinces on the geographic periphery of the country which occurred under the Ba'th is unique itself in the political history of the modern Middle East. The only countries in the Middle East which have come close to the Syrian achievement are Turkey and Egypt, both much larger and more homogeneous countries. As many examples in this book have indicated, the success and uniqueness of the Ba'th in Syria derives from its taking root in the rural provinces where the Ba'th socialist and secularist ideas, especially those entailing land reform, found a welcome audience. The strong appeal of Ba'thism to the rural population has been expressed in a much anthologized statement

of an Alawite military officer in 1970, the same
year that Hafiz al-Asad came to power: "Don't
expect us to eliminate socialism in Syria; for the
real meaning of such steps would be the transfer
of all the political, financial, industrial, and
commercial advantages to the towns, i.e. the
members of the Sunni community.   We, the
Alawis. . . , will then again be the poor and the
servants.   We shall not abandon socialism,
because it enables us to impoverish the
townspeople and to equalize their standard of life
to that of the villages."[46]

But what is more remarkable is that it is
doubtful whether the Alawis or other minorities
will again be the poor and servants, even if the
attachment to socialism dwindles; as, indeed, it
has in the last eleven years.

It must also be emphasized, as the studies of
Alasdair Drysdale, Raymond Hinnebusch and
Nikolaos Van Dam have indicated, that the
youthfulness of the Ba'th in the 1960's and their
generational homogeneity contributed greatly to
solidifying their ranks.   Another factor in the
success of the Ba'th regime was that most of them
were indigenously educated.   With the exception
of Iraq, where the same phenomenon has
occurred, this is a unique situation as far as
Middle Eastern and a good many other Third
World countries are concerned.   There have been
no studies to the knowledge of the writer on this
problem, but the case of Syria seems to indicate
that perhaps too many foreign educated among the
top decision-making elite of a developing country
may be detrimental to the stability of a regime
and the maintenance of the ideology which
sustains it.   However, evidence presented in this
book seems to indicate that the lack of
foreign--educated leaders in the economic sphere
is detrimental.   This point seems to be very clear

in Iraq.[47] The needs of a regime to retain power and ideological consistency seems to be more possible with a home--educated elite in power. But the economic needs of such a regime seem to need the input of foreign--educated technocrats. These contradictory needs of a developing country such as Syria, have not been adequately addressed by students of social change in Third World countries. This dichotomy of leadership training is even greater when rapid social change is taking place for that is when ethnic and religious sectarianism is at its height. We have some examples of this. The Iranian revolution attempted to place not only Muslims in power, but Iranian educated ones as well. This development[48] took place in Syria more than twenty years ago. It does bring the question to mind, however, that if Iran had had a completely home-educated decision-making elite, would it have been able to sustain itself more enduringly especially its economy while in the vortex of rapid social change?

In the nearly two decades of Ba'thist rule than, truly revolutionary changes have taken place in the altered relationship between center and periphery, among generations, sects and majority- minority groups. In reference to the Middle East as a whole, and possibly in a larger context, it raises the question of whether or not in a pluralistic or 'mosiac' society, such as Syria, a country can achieve more rapid development when led by minorities or some combination of minority groups rather than an entrenched, traditional majority?

The great success of the Syrian Ba'th during its first decade and a half of rule does not mean that it will be as successful in the 1980's. The major weaknesses of the regime are clear: it remains an authoritarian one-party state, which for reasons we have detailed, has failed to institutionalize its achievement. It is this failure which led to the large scale Islamic opposition against it in the late 1970's and early 1980's. In the view of the writer, however, the fact that the opposition was 'Islamic,' points again to the basic strengths of the regime. But it is also ominous for the future that many socio-economic groups which have not been Islamic- oriented traditionally have resorted to using Islam as a politial vehicle to redress their grievances. Furthermore as Ba'thism began to lose its own ideological and political energy in the late 1970's, it became even more authoritarian and increasingly prone to charges of sectarianism. This in turn prevented the inclusion in an institutionalized form of a broader spectrum of society. It has become increasingly a regime in paralysis. But the basic strengths of the regime allowed it to endure. Furthermore, the opposition in not yet enough strong to topple the regime. The Islamic opposition in Syria, unlike in Egypt, Iran and Algeria, does not, it seems, have a sufficiently strong nationalistic appeal. Many of the minorities, peasants, and even the salaried middle class tend to be unsympathetic to an opposition in league with rich landlords and merchants.[49]

It is also significant that much of the opposition to the al-Asad regime originated in the northern cities and particularly Aleppo and Hama traditionally more Islamic cities than Damascus. Aleppo was formerly a major stop on the famous silk road and until the twentieth century was commercially oriented to northern Iraq and even to the Anatolian towns of the Ottoman Empire. It was a major town of the Ottoman Empire and surpassed Damascus as a commercial center partly because of the rich farms in its hinterland. But

in the twentieth century, and this trend
continued under the Ba'th, Damascus became the
center of all government offices and the main
center of the country. This points up one of the
ironies, if not contradictions, of the Ba'thist
revolution during the past twenty years. Led by
a minority from the peripheral provinces which
had been exploited traditionally by the Sunnis of
Damascus, it has fostered through its own
centralization policies and location of party
headquarters there, even greater power in
Damascus. It is notable that Hafiz al-Asad upon
assuming power expanded the participation of
Damascenes in his government and that from 1966
to 1976 while four members of the Regional
Command came from Damascus, not a single one
came from Aleppo![50] In the eyes of the people of
Aleppo, their city was being relegated to that of
a mere provincial capital on a level with Latakia.
This feat was being accomplished by a
minority-led government which, in spite of the
fact that they had been exploited historically in
every conceivable way by Damascus, obviously
felt more akin to Damascus than to any other
city. Moreover, as noted above, it was Damascus
which was the seat of much of the unrest against
the al-Jadid regime. In short, while the Ba'thist
revolution led to a major increase in the political
power of the periphery, there has not been much
of a reorientation of the physical resources of the
country, with the exception that there is now a
university in Latakia. Thus, in spite of the
depth of the Ba'thist revolution in Syria, that
country still exhibits many of the characteristics
of other Middle Eastern and Third World countries
and that is a kind of internal imperialism of the
rest of the country by the major city or cities of
the country.
    The major problem facing the Ba'th regime in

Syria in the 1980's is that of Lebanon. Syria has now been in Lebanon for almost six years. The 'Greater Lebanon' of post-World War I has been destroyed, possibly to the gain of a 'Greater Syria.' But the restrictions are great. It seems unlikely that Israel or the United States will permit Syria to consolidate her control over Lebanon short of total acquiescence to the Israeli annexation of the West Bank or, at least, effective Israeli control of the West Bank, the Gaza Strip and, perhaps Southern Lebanon. This would leave the Palestinians in Lebanon. Even if the United States begins to negotiate with the PLO with Syrian consent, as the mission of Philip Habib in July 1981 seemed to indicate, the negotiations would be extrememly drawn out and its is highly unlikely that anything of territorial consequence would be achieved before the end of the 1980's. The room that Syria has to maneuver in is therefore very limited because of Maronite, Palestinian and particularly U.S.-backed Israeli pressures. Even if Hafiz al-Asad stays in power to 1985 or so, his direction of the country, despite the Islamic opposition and all that it entails, will be dictated largely by events in Lebanon which are now so closely tied to the Palestinian question, the Arab-Israeli conflict and American interests, not to mention Israeli interests in the Middle East. The serious stagnation of Ba'thist ideology, the inability to broaden further the Ba'thist base of power and to institutionalize even one-party rule will limit further vital developments in the 1980's. But these eventualities should not obscure the great achievements of the Ba'th and the changes which have occurred in Syria during the two decades of Ba'thist rule. From a militantly pan-Arab ideology it evolved into a centralized one-party, authoritian state which was able to accomplish the alteration of Syria for the first time in its political history into a nation-state as that word is usually understood in the West. Whether or not the Syrian state will be consolidated further remains to be seen. But if some 'accomodating' solution is not found to the 'Palestinian Question' and to the 'Lebanese Conflict,' then the consolidation achieved by the Ba'th and the 'state-building' achievements of the Ba'th in Syria during the past two decades may be undone, and Syria, too, may fall prey to 'destabilization,' which is so often exploited by Israel, the United States and the Soviet Union.

In summary then this study has attempted to answer the question whether an ethnically or religiously minoritarian regime can facilitate, as quickly or more quickly, the process of modernization than a majoritarian regime and, secondly, if this modernization can be accompanied by political development. The case of Syria has shown that modernization has proceeded rapidly under the Ba'th regime from the 1960's onward and that it continued to advance rapidly after the Ba'th civilian and military systems came to be dominated almost exclusively by Alawites. The most rapid modernization came about from the middle of the 1960's to 1975-6. The latter date marks direct Syrian intervention into Lebanon. Would Syria have progressed as rapidly under a Sunni-dominated government during the same time span? The conclusion of this study is that it would probably not have done so. While it is true that certain sectors of the economy under a non-Alawite regime may have developed more rapidly, it is unlikely that the uniformity of development and resource allocation, especially in the peripherial provinces, would have been achieved. It must be stressed, however, that the achievements of the minoritarian regimes of the Alawites, especially of Salah al-Jadid and Hafiz al-Asad, were in conjunction with the ideology of Ba'thism and the authoritarian one party system upon which they were based.

The interesting question then of whether or not modernization in an ethnically or religiously pluralistic or 'mosaic' country can be facilitated by a geographically peripheral ethnic or religious minoritarian government as quickly or more quickly than by a majoritarian government must be answered positively. In the case of Syria this is true up to 1975-6.

The second part of the question as to whether or not political development will accompany or could proceed along with modernization is a more difficult question. By political development here is meant the increasing of the political enfranchisement of more individuals representative of the diverse groups of which the country is comprised. As this study has shown, particularly as represented by Drysdale's data, the greater enfranchisement of the Sunnis in meaningful ways was taking place during the first five years of Hafiz al-Asad's rule. Also, even though the Isma'ili's and Druzes had not retained the leadership positions they had occupied in the early years of Ba'th rule, they were present in lesser positions. However, the opportunities for political development decreased drastically after 1976 and this was due to a large extent, but not absolutely to the intervention and involvement of Syria in Lebanon with all of the consequences that this entailed, many of which are still unfolding and new ones being created.

This situation poses another observation for the politics of an ethnically or religiously minoritarian regime and that is that while in the early stages, modernization as represented by a new regime-especially when the ideology accompanying the revolution or the regime has extra-minoritarian appeal-can proceed apace without political development, modernization will encounter great difficulties and the necessary dynamics between economic modernization and political development will reach an impasse. In this regard a regime of an ethnic or religious minority, as defined in this study, differs substantially from an ideological class and/or elite-dominated government of a minority in a more homogeneous society or in a society in which the ethnic and religious lines are more blurred or less important than in the case of Syria.

It would have been interesting from a historical point of view and from the point of view of a political scientist to have seen what would have evolved in Syria without the pervading questions of the 'Palestinian=Lebanese' problems. It is quite possible that the regime of Hafiz al-Asad or an Alawite-dominated regime might have continued into the 1990's, a possibility which is now highly unlikely. Then the questions raised in this study would have been able to be answered more definitely. Perhaps some kind of Alawite-Sunni compatible compromise would have been obtained. However, after 1976 it became clear that this was not going to occur. After 1976 it became increasingly necessary for the al-Asad regime to curtail the enlargement of political enfranchisement in order to insure the survivability of his regime and, indeed, of Ba'thism, from attack not only from internal opposition, but from Palestinians and Lebanese of both the left and right – Muslim and Christian. The opposition was increased dramatically by the rise of the 'Islamic opposition' at home which reached the level of civil war in 1980. Serious opposition continued throughout 1981 by all groups and is likely to continue.

The annexation of the Golan Heights by Israel on 14 December, 1981 although probably inevitable as a result of the expansionist policies pursued by Israel for the last fourteen years, points out even more dramatically the multiplying dilemmas of the al-Asad regime.   Although it is difficult to determine whether or not Syria would have retaliated militarily to the annexation of the Golan Heights, it seems certain that her involvement in Lebanon precluded her from doing so.   Thus Syria's intervention has placed the al-Asad regime in even more straitened circumstances for now it will have to respond to an even stronger and more bellicose Israel, in addition to opponents in Lebanon and the 'Islamic opposition' at home.   It is difficult to see how the al-Asad regime can respond, even piecemeal to these challenges without a further serious deterioration in the legitimacy of the regime.   The only viable response would seem to be war, but if this were to be the case, more than Syria, Lebanon or Israel would be involved.   Even if a re-run of the 1973 war were to occur it is difficult to see how this would result in the strengthening of al-Asad's regime.   Indeed, if this scenario were to occur Ba'thism itself and the ideological role that it has played in the evolution of party and state in Syria would be threatened. As the Al-Asad regime begins its twelfth year in power in 1982, Ba'thism in Syria has become a diminished political force and threatened ideology in a partially paralyzed state.

FOOTNOTES

CHAPTER I

THE IDEOLOGY OF THE BA'TH

[1]Petran, 89; Seale, 149-51; Torrey[2], 448.[*]

[2]Haim[2], 134.

[3]Ibid., 134-

[4]Kaylani, 6; Seale, 155.

[5]Kaylani, 6-7.

[6]Ibid., 7.

[7]Ibid., 5.

[8]Aflaq, Fi Sabil al-Ba'th (1963), 181.

[9]Aflaq, Arakat al-Masir al-Wahid (1958), 19; Cf. also art. 'Wakf,' in H.A.R. Gibb and J. H. Kramers, eds., Shorter Encyclopaedia of Islam(Leiden, London, 1953), pp. 624-628.

[10]Abu Jaber, 101.

[11]Petran, 90.

[12]Achmucker, 51-62. The following page or so is based on Schmucker's analysis.

[13]Ibid.

[*]Numbers in superscript after an author's name mean that the note refers to the second work listed under the author's name in the bibliography. When an author has more than two

works, an abbreviated version of the title is given.

[14] Ibid., 89-90.

[15] Seale, 154.

[16] Ibid.

[17] Petran, 90.

[18] Aflaq, Fi Sabil (1959), 209-10.

[19] Aflaq, Fi Sabil (1963), 332.   (Quoted in Kaylani, 6).

[20] Seale, 157.

[21] Petran, 90.

[22] Torrey[2], 451.

[23] Aflaq, Fi Sabil (1963), 219-23.

[24] Aflaq, Fi Sabil (1959), 96-8.

[25] Ibid., 98.

[26] Ibid.

[27] Ibid., 99-100.

[28] Torrey[2], 449.

[29] Petran, 90.

[30] Aflaq, Fi Sabil (1963), 123-4.

[31] Petran, 237.

[32] Ibid., 91.

[33] Kinnane, 32-3.

[34] Petran, 236-7.

[35] Personal communication with Professor Ihsan Abbas of the American University of Beirut and Princeton University.

[36] Aflaq, Nuqtah al-Bidayah, 105-6.

[37] Ben-Tzur, 170.

[38] Ibid., 169-70.

[39] Ibid., 170.

[40] Ibid., 170-1.

[41] Ibid., 171.

[42] Ibid., 172-3.

[43] Ibid., 173-4.

[44] Ibid., 174.

[45] Ibid.

[46] Ibid., 174-5.

[47] Ibid., 175-6.

[48] Ibid., 176.

CHAPTER II

ORIGINS AND EARLY YEARS OF THE BA'TH
IN SYRIA

[1] Seale, 149-51; Torrey[2], 448.

[2] Aflaq, al-Qawmiyya al-'Arabiyya wa Lik ti fatuha
min al-Shuyu'iyya (Arab Nationalism and Its
Differences from Communism), Damascus,
1944.

[3] Seale, 151.

[4] Kaylani, 8; Petran, 89, 91.

[5] Petran, 92; Seale, 151-2.

[6] Petran, 93; Seale, 151-2.

[7] Petran, 95-6; Cf. also, Miles Copeland, The
Game
of Nations(N.Y., 1957), passim.

[8] Ibid., 96; for further details Cf. R. B. Winder,
"Syrian Deputies and Cabinet Ministers,
1919-1959," M.E.J. 16(1962) pp. 407-429 and
17(1963), pp. 35-54.

[9] Ibid., 102.

[10] Ibid., 103.

[11] Kaylani, 13; Petran, 104.

[12] Petran, 104.

[13] Ibid., 104-5.

[14] Kaylani, 15-6; Petran, 106.

[15] Petran, 107; Seale, 176-7.

[16] Seale, 177.

[17] Petran, 104.

[18] Petran, 107-8; Seale, 182.

[19] Seale, 182-4.

[20] Petran, 108-10; Seale, 214-6, 219.

[21] Petran, 110; Seale, 219.

[22] Petran, 110; Seale, 220, 236-7.

[23] Seale, 237.

[24] Petran, 110; Seale, 239-43.

[25] Petran, 115; Seale, 115-6.

[26] Petran, 115-6.

[27] Ibid., 122-4.

[28] Petran, 121-5; Rabinovich, 14-5.

CHAPTER III

UNION AND SECESSION

[1]Petran, 125.

[2]Kerr, 11-12.

[3]Kerr, 12; Petran, 129.

[4]Petran, 129; Rabinovich, 17.

[5]Petran, 121-2.

[6]Kerr, 14; Petran, 133-4; Rabinovich, 17.

[7]Petran, 124-5; Rabinovich, 22.

[8]Kerr, 16-19; Petran, 135; Rabinovich, 17-8.

[9]Petran, 146.

[10]Ibid., 149-50.

[11]Kerr^2, 691-2.

[12]Rabinovich, 22.

[13]Petran, 150-1.

[14]Kerr, 22; Petran, 153.

[15]Petran, 155-7; Rabinovich, 30-3.

[16]Petran, 157-8; Rabinovich, 33-4.

[17]Rabinovich, 36-9.

[18]Ibid., 39.

[19]Ibid., 40-2.

[20]Petran, 158-60.

[21]Macdonald, 370-1; Petran, 161.

[22]Kerr, 44; Petran, 164-5; Rabinovich, 43-9.

CHAPTER IV

TRADITIONAL SYRIA BEFORE THE BA'TH

[1]Hinnebusch, "Party and Peasant," 2-8. See bibliographical note.

[2]Ibid.; Andre Latron, 222-5; also, Hinnebusch, "Rural Politics," 279-80.

[3]Hinnebusch, 9.

[4]Ibid., 11.

[5]Harik, 30-41.

CHAPTER V

THE ROLE OF THE MINORITIES IN THE BA'TH:
ALAWITES, DRUZE, AND ISMA'ILIS

[1] Hreib.

[2] Harik, Politics, and Polk, The Opening, deal extensively with these developments.

[3] Salibi, 80-119; Tibawi, 121-47.

[4] Shamir, 347-75.

[5] Howard. The entire book should be consulted.

[6] Hourani, 163-229; Longrigg, 104-333.

[7] Cited in Hreib, 164.

[8] Haddad, 45.

[9] This paragraph is taken from Hreib, 166.

[10] Ibid., 168.

[11] Gubser, 114, quoted in Hreib, 168.

CHAPTER VI

THE BA'TH IN POWER: 1963-1966

[1] Kerr, 44; Nyrop, 153-4; Petran, 167.

[2] Kerr, 45; Petran, 165; Rabinovich, 52-4.

[3] Rabinovich, 54.

[4] Nyrop, 154; Rabinovich, 54.

[5] Rabinovich, 55-6.

[6] Kerr, 48.

[7] Kerr, 58, 69-71; Rabinovich, 65-70.

[8] Kerr, 81; Rabinovich, 64-5.

[9] Kerr, 82.

[10] Kerr, 81-5; Rabinovich, 65-9.

[11] Kerr, 87-8; Rabinovich, 69-70.

[12] Ibid.

[13] Rabinovich, 75-80.

[14] Ibid., 80-90.

[15] Petran, 173; Rabinovich, 94-5.

[16] Petran, 173-4; Rabinovich, 95.

[17] Rabinovich, 96-9.

[18] Ibid., 99-100.

[19] Kerr, 99-100; Petran, 191-2; Rabinovich, 101.

[20] Rabinovich, 101-2.

[21] Petran, 174; Rabinovich, 103-4.

[22] Rabinovich, 104.

[23] Ibid., 105-7.

[24] Ibid., 107.

[25] Petran, 174-5; Rabinovich, 109-15.

[26] Kerr, 104-5.

[27] Petran, 176-7; Rabinovich, 112.

[28] Rabinovich, 121.

[29] Ibid., 125-32.

[30] Ibid., 132-3.

[31] Petran, 177-8; Rabinovich, 133.

[32] Rabinovich, 133-5.

[33] Petran, 178; Rabinovich, 135-9.

[34] Petran, 178; Rabinovich, 139-40.

[35] Petran, 178-9; Rabinovich, 140-3.

[36] Rabinovich, 145-7.

[37] Ibid., 148.

[38] Ibid., 148-156.

[39] Petran, 180; Rabinovich, 156-7.

[40] Rabinovich, 158.

[41] Munif   ar   Razzaz,   al-Tajriba   al-Murra   (The Bitter
      Experience), Beirut, 167, 142.   (In
      Rabinovich, 158).

[42] Rabinovich, 159.

[43] Petran, 180; Rabinovich, 160-1.

[44] Rabinovich, 161-4.

[45] Petran, 180; Rabinovich, 165.   (I have followed
      Rabinovich's chronology, which differs
      somewhat from that of Petran).

[46] Rabinovich, 167-70.

[47] Ibid., 170.

[48] Ibid., 170-1.

[49] Petran, 180; Rabinovich, 176-9.

[50] Rabinovich, 180-2.

[51] Ibid., 182.

[52] Ibid., 182-3.

[53] Petran, 180-1; Rabinovich, 183-4.

[54] Rabinovich, 184.

[55] Ibid.

[56]Petran, 181; Rabinovich, 184.

[57]Petran, 181; Rabinovich, 185.

[58]Rabinovich, 186-7.

[59]Ibid.

[60]Petran, 181; Rabinovich, 186.

[61]Rabinovich, 186-91.

[62]Ibid., 191.

[63]Ibid., 191-2.

[64]Ibid., 192.

[65]Petran, 181; Rabinovich, 191.

[66]Pteran, 181; Rabinovich, 191.

[67]Petran, 181-2; Rabinovich, 193-5.

[68]Rabinovich, 195.

[69]Petran, 182; Rabinovich, 196.

[70]Rabinovich, 196-7.

[71]Ibid., 197.

[72]Ibid., 198-200.

[73]Petran, 182; Rabinovich, 201-2.

CHAPTER VII

THE NEO-BA'TH: 1966-1970

[1]Kerr, 120; Petran, 182; Rabinovich, 202.

[2]Kerr, 120; Petran, 182; Rabinovich, 203-4.

[3]Kerr, 120; Petran, 182; Rabinovich, 204-5.

[4]Rabinovich, 209.

[5]Ibid., 210-11.

[6]Schmucker, 146-80; the next few paragraphs rely
    on Schmucker.

[7]Kerr[2], 693-4.

[8]Kerr, 121-2.

[9]Kerr, 122; Kerr[2], 696.

[10]Kimche, 48-9; Draper, 38-9n.

[11]Kraper, 34; Jabbar, 167; Petran, 195.

[12]Jabbar, 160-1.

[13]Kimche, 23; Petran, 195-6.

[14]Jabbar, 168-9; Kimche, 23-4.

[15]Kimche, 24.

[16]Petran, 196-7.

[17]Ibid., 197-8.

[18] Kerr, 126-7; Kerr^2, 696.

[19] Kerr, 127.

[20] Ibid., 127-8.

[21] Kimche, 108.

[22] Ibid.

[23] Petran, 199.

[24] Kerr, 129; Kerr^2, 697.

[25] Petran, 201.

[26] Kimche, 243; Petran, 201; Vatikiotis, 239.

[27] Petran, 202-3.

[28] Ibid., 203.

[29] Ibid., 203-5.

[30] Ibid., 209.

[31] Ibid., 205-16.

[32] Ibid., 218-33.

[33] Ibid., 239.

[34] Kimche, 258-9.

[35] Kerr^2, 698; Petran, 239-40.

[36] Kimche, 259; Petran, 241; Quandt, 64.

[37] Petran, 241.

[38] Ibid., 242.

[39] Kerr^2, 698; Petran, 242-3.

[40] Kerr^2, 698.

[41] Kerr^2, 149; Kerr^2, 698-9; Nyrop, 176.

[42] Kerr^2, 699.   (Asad is quoted by Kerr from the
English edition of Le Monde, 18 November
1970).

CHAPTER VIII

ASAD IN CONTROL:
THE CONSOLIDATION OF THE REGIME,
1970-1975

[1] All of these quotes are from Van Dam, The Struggle for Power in Syria, 93.

[2] Van Dam, "Middle East Political Cliches," 42.

[3] Hinnebusch, "The Islamic Movement in Syria," 207.

[4] Drysdale, "The Syrian Armed Forces," 30; Petran 235.

[5] Ibid., 30.

[6] Hinnebusch, "The Islamic Movement in Syria," 207.

[7] Drysdale, "The Syrian Armed Forces," 31.

[8] Nikolaos Van Dam had stated than, "After the November coup in particular, rumours circulating in the country and outside its borders suggested that rivalry between the two brothers and even that from time to time, Rif'at had threatened his brother's position. Thus, when the army reportedly attempted to transfer him and his units away from Damascus, it was rumoured that Rif'at had repeatedly revolted." See The Struggle for Power in Syria, 90-1. I have not been able to confirm the truth of this statement from any other source and it should be noted that Van Dam's source, ft. 28 indicates that his information came from al-Rayah, a pro-Jadid

newspaper in Beirut.

[9] Van Dam's entire essay contains the theme that if a coup d'etat were to occur, because of Alawite dominance of the military process and of the security systems, it would be by other Alawites and probably not by Sunnis.

[10] Ibid., 89.

[11] Drysdale, "The Syrian Armed Forces," 32.

[12] Van Dam, The Struggle for Power in Syria, 84.

[13] Hinnebusch, "The Islamic Movement in Syria," explanatory note D, 242.

[14] For a detailed explanation of the governmental structure of Syria under Asad, the reader should consult John Devlin, Syria: A Country Profile (Westview Press, 1982), chapter 6,10. This is the tentative title of the study and I quote from the xerox copy which the author supplied me.

[15] Kerr[2], 703.

[16] Petran, 250-1.

[17] This is especially true in the relevant works of Devlin and Hinnebusch.

[18] Drysdale, "The Syrian Political Elite," 3-30. The account which follows is based on Drysdale's study.

[19] Ibid., 12.

[20] Ibid., 13.

[21] Ibid.

[22] Ibid., 14.

[23] Ibid., 21.

[24] Ibid., 24.

[25] Ibid.

[26] Dawisha, "Syria under Asad.". The following several paragraphs are based on Dawisha's article. Also see Olson, "The Ba'th in Syria," 464-7.

[27] Kerr^2, 701-2.

[28] Ibid., Nyrop, 169.

[29] Ibid., 169; 177.

[30] Kerr^2, 705.

[31] Laqueur, 46; 54-9.

[32] Ibid., 110-11.

[33] Laqueur, 46, 54-9.

[34] Ibid., 101, 104-5, 110.

[35] Ibid., 110-11.

CHAPTER IX

THE MODERATION OF IDEOLOGY AND
THE EVOLUTION OF PARTY AND STATE
UNDER ASAD:

1975-1981

[1]Van Dam, "Middle Eastern Political Cliches," 54.

[2]Ibid., 56.

[3]Dawisha, "Syria in Lebanon," and "Syria's
Intervention in Lebanon." Both of these
articles are similar in content. The one in
The Jerusalem Journal of International
Relations is geared to a systems analysis of
12 crucial decisions which the Syrians had to
make. The reader should also consult Galia
Golan, "Syria and the Soviet Union since the
Yom Kippur War;" Ilana Kass, "Moscow and the
Lebanese Triangle;" Robert Freedman, "The
Soviet Union and the Civil War in Lebanon."
The best of these articles is the one by
Kass. All of the articles agree that Syria
was able to pursue its perceived interests in
opposition to those desired by the Soviet
Union.

[4]Ajami, "The End of Pan-Arabism," 355-73.

[5]Dawisha, "Syria in Lebanon," 144-5.

[6]For a review of some current literature on ethnic
conflict in the Middle East see John Entelis'
review of six books which deal with this
topic in Polity, II, No. 3 (Spring 1979),
400-10.

[7]According to Walid Khalidi.

[8]There are several books on the Lebanese civil
war.   Among the best as of 1981 are those
by Walid Khalidi, Kamal Salibi and Marius
Deeb listed in the bibliography.

[9]Khalidi, 76.

[10]Ibid.   For a good survey of the major actors in
the Lebanese civil war see Deeb, 21-119.

[11]Deeb, 51.

[12]Ibid.

[13]Quoted in full from Khalidi, 83.

[14]Ibid., 87.

[15]Ibid.

[16]Dan Tschirgi, The Christian Science Monitor, 16
July 1981.

[17]Ibid.

[18]A bibliography bringing the literature on the
'Islamic Revival' up to date can be found in
Ibrahim,   449   and   Akhavi,   "Shi'i   Social
Thought   and   Praxis   in   Recent   Iranian
History,"   195-8.

[19]Dessouki, Introduction, 6-7.   I quote from the
xerox copy which the author sent me.

[20]Ibid., 7-8.

[21]Ibrahim, 443-53 and Ayubi, 481-99.

[22]Ibrahim, 447.

[23] Ibid., 449.

[24] Hinnebusch, "The Islamic Movement in Syria,"
201. The four factors which I mention here
are quoted and paraphrased from
Hinnebusch's article.

[25] Ibid., 203.

[26] Hinnebusch, "Political Recruitment and
Socialization in Syria," 153.

[27] Ibid., 156.

[28] Ibid., 158.

[29] Ibid., 168.

[30] Ibid.

[31] Ibid., 170.

[32] Ibid.

[33] Hinnebusch, "The Islamic Movement in Syria,"
223.

[34] Christian Science Monitor, 27 June 1979.

[35] For a detailed account of these events see
Hinnebusch, "The Islamic Movement in Syria,"
239.

[36] For a full text see British Broadcasting
Corporation, Survey of World Broadcasts, Part
IV: The Middle East, Me/5185/A/6-7, 14 April
1976. I found this reference in Dawisha,
"Syria under Asad," 345, ft. 8.

[37] Kelidar, 20.

[38] Ibid., 21.

[39] Ibid., 22.

[40] Lebanon News, II, No. 6 (June 1979), 1.

[41] Le Monde, 4 June 1976. The interviewer was Eric Rouleau.

[42] Springbord, 193-4.

[43] See the works of Marr, Khadduri, Penrose, Olson and Springbord in the bibliography.

[44] Christian Science Monitor, 25 June 1981, page 9.

[45] Springbord, 193-207.

[46] Be'eri, 337.

[47] Springbord, 206-7.

[48] This statement does mean that I think the Iranian revolution will be successful like the Syrian Ba'th revolution. But the role of a foreign educated elite was much larger and more important than that of their colleagues in Syria and Iraq. Also the role of the foreign educated is greater in Syria than in Iraq, especially in the agricultural sector. For a comparison of the two countries' agricultural policies, see Springbord, 193-207.

[49] Hinnebusch, "The Islamic Movement in Syria," 241.

[50] Drysdale, "The Syrian Political Elite," 8.

BIBLIOGRAPHY

Aflaq, Michael, al-Ba'th wa al-Wadah (The Ba'th and Unity). Al-Mu'assas al-'Arabiya li'l-Dirasat wa'l-Nashr, Beirut, 1974.

_____, Fi Sabil al-Ba'th (For the Sake of the Ba'th). Dar al-Taliah li'l-Tiba'ah wa'l-Nashr, Beirut, 1959.

_____, Fi Sabil al-Ba'th. Dar al-Taliah li'l-Tiba'ah wa'l-Nashr, Beirut, 1964 (second edition).

_____, Ma'rakat al'Masir al-Wahid (The Struggle of One Destiny). Dar al-Arab, Beirut, 1958.

_____, Mar'rakat al-Masir al-Wahid. Al-Mu'assasa al-'Arabiya li'l-Dirasa wa'l-Nashr, Beirut, 1972 (Fourth edition).

_____, Nuqtah al-Bidayah (The Starting Point). Al-Mu'assasa al-'Arabiya li'l-Dirasa wa'l-Nashr, Beirut, 1971.

Abu Jaber, Kamil S., The Arab Ba'th Socialist Party. Syracuse: Syracuse University Press, N.Y., 1966.

Ajami, Fuad, "The End of Pan-Arabism," Foreign Affairs, vol. 57 (Winter 1978-79), 355-73.

Akhavi, Shahrough, Religion and Politics in Contemporary Iran: Clergy-State Relations in the Pahlavi Period. Albany: State University of New York Press, 1980.

_____, "Shi'i Social Thought and Praxis

in Recent Iranian History," in Islam in the Contemporary World ed. Cyriac K. Pullapilly (Notre Dame: Indiana, 1980), 171-99.

Al-Nazeer, A news sheet published in Damascus by Al-Mujahideen in Syria.

Ayubi, Nazih N., "The Political Revival of Islam: The Case of Egypt," International Journal of Middle East Studies, 12, No. 4 (December 1980), 481-99.

Beieri, Eliezer, Army Officers in Arab Politics and Society, trans. Dov Ben-Abba. New York: Praeger, 1970.

Ben-Tzur, Avraham, "The Neo-Ba'th Party of Syria," Journal of Contemporary History, Institute of Contemporary History, London Vol. 3, No. 3, (1968), 161-181.

Dawisha, A., "Syria Under Asad, 1970-78: The Centres of Power," Government and Opposition, 13, No. 3 (1978), 341-54.

_____, "Syria in Lebanon: Asad's Vietnam," Foreign Policy, No. 3 (Winter 1978-79), 135-50.

_____, "The Transnational Party in Regional Politics: The Arab Ba'th Party," Asian Affairs, Vol. 61 (1974), 23-31.

_____, "Syria's Intervention in Lebanon, 1975-76," The Jerusalem Journal of International Relations, Vol.3, No. 2-3 (Winter-Spring 1978), 245-64.

Dessouki, Ali E. Hillah, and Alexander S. Cudsi,

Islam and Power in the Contemporary Muslim
World.   Baltimore   and   London: John
Hopkins University Press, 1981.

_____, Islamic Resurgence in the Arab
World.   New York: Praeger, 1982.

Devlin, John, Syria: A Country Profile.
        Boulder Colorado: Westview Press, 1982. I
        used chapter six, seven and eight of this
        study from xerox copies which the author
        sent to me.

_____, The Ba'th Party: A History from
its Origins to 1966.   Stanford, California:
Hoover Institution Press; 1976.

Draper, Theodore, Israel and World Politics. New
        York: The Viking Press, 1968.

Drysdale, Alasdair, "Ethnicity in the Syrian
        Officer   Corps: A   Conceptualization,"
        Civilizations, 29 (1979), 359-73.

_____, "Syria's Troubled Ba'thi Regime,"
Current   History,   80,   No.   462   (January
1981), 32-43.

_____, "The Regional Equalization of
Health Care and Education in Syria since the
Ba'thi Revolution," International Journal of
Middle East Studies, 13, No. 1 (February
1981), 93-111.

_____,"The Syrian Armed Forces in
National   Politics: The   Role   of   the
Geographic   and   Ethnic   Periphery,"   in
Soldiers, Peasants and Bureaucrats, ed.
Andrzej   Korbonski   and   Roman   Kalkovicz.

London: Allen and Unwin, 1982.

_____,"The Syrian Political Elite
1966-1976: A Spatial and Social Analysis,"
Middle Eastern Studies, 17, No. 2 (April
1981), 3-30.

Entelis, John, review articles in polity, XI, No.
3 (Spring 1979), 400-10.

Freedman, Robert O., "The Soviet Union and the
Civil War in Lebanon, 1975-76," in The
Jerusalem Journal of International Relations,
Vol. 3, No. 4 (Summer 1978), 60-93.

Gubser, Peter, The United Arab Republic: A
Study in Unity, Master's thesis. Beirut:
American University of Beirut, 1966.

_____, "Minorities in Power: The
Alawites of Syria," in The Political Role of
Minority Groups in the Middle East ed. R.D.
McLaurin (Praeger, 1979), 17-49.

Golan, Galia, "Syria and the Soviet Union since
the Yom Kippur War," in Orbis, Vol. 21,
No. 4 (Winter 1978), 777-802.

Haddad, George, Revolutions and Military Rule in
the Middle East, three volumes. New York:
R. Speller, 1971.

Haim, Sylvia, Arab Nationalism: An Anthology,
Berkeley: University of California Press,
1962.

_____, "The Ba'th in Syria," People and
Politics in the Middle East, ed. Michael
Curtis. New Brunswick, N.J., Transaction

Books (1971), 132-143.

Harik, Iliya, "An Approach to the Study of
    Middle Eastern Politics," in Middle East
    Studies Association Bulletin, Vol. 4, No. 1
    (February 15, 1970), 30-41. The section on
    mobilization is taken from this work with the
    permission of Professor Harik.

_____, Politics and Change in a
    Traditional   Society: Lebanon,   1711-1845.
    Princeton: Princeton   University   Press,
    1968.

Heikal, Mohamed, The Road to Ramadan. New
    York: Quadrangle Press, 1975.

Hinnebusch, Raymond, "Party and Peasant in
    Syria: Rural Politics and Social Change in a
    Mobilizational   Regime: Organization   and
    Mobilization   in   Four   Village   Cases,"   paper
    presented   at   the   1975   convention   of   the
    Middle East Studies Association, Louisville,
    Ky.   Sections of this study appear in "Local
    Politics   in   Syria: Organization   and
    Mobilization   in   Four   Villages,   "The   Middle
    East Journal, Vol. 30, No. 1 (Winter, 1976),
    1-23.   Professor Hinnebusch did field work
    in Syria in 1973-74 and this is one of the
    first studies in many years to be based on
    first   hand   field   data.   The   section   on
    'Traditional   Syria   before   the   Ba'th'   relies
    heavily on his paper and is used with his
    permission.

_____, "Rural politics in Ba'thist Syria:
    A Case Study in the Role of the Countryside
    in   the   Political   Development   of   Arab
    Societies," in Saad E. Ibrahim and Nicolas

Hopkins, eds., Arab Society in Transition:
A Reader, Cairo, Egypt (1977), 278-95.

_____, "Political Recruitment and Social-
ization in Syria: The Case of the
Revolutionary Youth Federation," in International Journal of Middle East Studies, 11,
No. 2 (April 1980), 43-74.

_____, "The Islamic Movement in Syria:
Sectarian Conflict and Urban Rebellion in an
Authoritarian Populist Regime," in Islamic
Resurgence in the Arab World, edited by Ali
E. Hillal Dessouki dealing with the
contemporary Islamic movements in the Middle
East. I used the xerox copy sent to me by
Professor Dessouki. The book will be
published by Praeger.

Hourani, Albert, Arabic Thought in the Liberal
Age, 1798-1939.   New York: Oxford
University Press, 1970.

_____, Syria and Lebanon, A Political
Essay. London: Oxford University Press,
1940.

Howard Harry N., The King-Crane Commission,
An American Inquiry in the Middle East.
Beirut: Khayats, 1963.

Hreib, Aleddin Saleh, "The Influence of
Sub-Regionalism (Rural Areas) on the
Structure of Syrian Politics 1920-1973."
Unpublished PH.D. Dissertation, Georgetown
University, 1976. Some material for the
section, "The Role of the Minorities in the
Ba'th arty," was taken from Hreib's work.

Hudson, Michael, "The Lebanese Crisis: The
    Limits of Consociational Democracy," Journal
    of Palestine Studies, Vol. 5, No. 3-4
    (Spring-Summer 1976), 109-22.

_____, "The Palestinian Factor in the
    Lebanese Civil War," The Middle East
    Journal, Vol. 32 (Summer 1978), 261-78.

Ibrahim, Saad Eddin, "Anatomy of Egypt's Militant
    Islamic Groups: Methodological note and
    Preliminary Findings," in International
    Journal of Middle East Studies, 12 No. 4
    (December 1980) 423-53.

Jabbar, Fuad, "The Palestinian Resistance and
    Inter-Arab Politics," in The Politics of
    Palestinian Nationalism, ed. William B.
    Quandt, Los Angeles: University of
    California Press (1974), 155-216.

Jureidini, Paul A. and R.D. McLaurin, Beyond
    Camp David: Emerging Alignments and
    Leaders in the Middle East.   Syracuse:
    Syracuse University Press 1981.

Karpat, Kemal H., ed., Political and Social
    Thought in the Contemporary Middle East.
    New York: Praeger, 1970.

Kass, Ilana, "Moscow and the Lebanese Triangle,"
    The Middle East Journal, 33 No. 2 (Spring
    1979), 169-88.

Kaylani, Nabil M., "The Rise of the Syrian Ba'th,
    1940-1958:   Political Success, Party Failure,"
    International Journal of Middle East Studies,
    Vol. 3, No. 1 (1972), 3-22.

Kelidar, A.R., "Religion and State in Syria,"
    Asian Affairs, Vol. 61, Part I (February
    1974), 16-22.

Kerr, Malcolm H., The Arab Cold War, New York:
    Oxford University Press, 1971.

_____, "Hafiz Asad and the Changing
    Patterns of Syrian Politics," International
    Journal, No. 4 (Autumn 1973), 689-707.

Khadduri, Majid, Socialist Iraq: A Study in
    Iraqi Politics Since 1968. Washington, D.C.:
    The Middle East Institute, 1978.

_____, Political Trends in the Arab
    World. Baltimore: The Johns Hopkins Press,
    1970.

Khalidi, Walid, Conflict and Violence in Lebanon:
    Confrontation   in   the   Middle   East.
    Cambridge: Harvard University Press, 1979.

Khouri, Fred J., The Arab-Israeli Dilemma.
    Syracuse: Syracuse University Press, 1973.

Kimche, David, and Dan Bawly, The Sandstorm.
    New York : Stein and Day, 1968.

Kinnane, Derk, The Kurds and Kurdistan.
    London: Oxford University Press, 1970.

Laqueur, Walter, Confrontation, New York:
    Bantam Books, 1974.

Latron, A., La vie rurale en Syrie et au Liban.
    Beyrouth, 1936.

Lenczowski, George., "Socialism in Syria," in

Helen   Desfasses   and   Jacques   Sevesque,
eds.,   Socialism   in   the   Third   World,   New
York: Praeger Publishers,   (1975),   55-76.

Longrigg, Stephen H.,   Syria and Lebanon under
French Mandate.   London: Oxford University
Press, 1958.

Macdonald,   Robert   W.,   The League of Arab
States.   Princeton: Princeton   University
Press, 1965.

Ma'oz, Moshe,   "Alawi Military Officers in Syrian
Politics: 1966-1974,"   in   Military and State   in
Modern   Asia,   ed.   Harold   Z.   Schriffren
(Jerusalem, 1976), 277-98.

Marr, Phebe,   "Iraq" in George Lenczowski,
Political Elites in the Middle East.   American
Enterprise   Institute: Washington,   D.C.
(1975), 109-49.

_____, "Iraq's Leadership Dilemma: A
Study   in   Leadership   Trends,   1948-1968,"
The   Middle East Journal,   Vol. 24,   No. 3
(Summer 1970), 283-301.

_____, "The Ba'th Party in Iraq."   Paper
presented   at   the   annual   meeting   of   the
Middle East Studies Association, Ann Arbor,
Michigan, November 11-14, 1978.

_____, "The Iraqi Revolution, A Case
Study of Army Rule," Orbis, Vol. XIV, No.
3 (1970), 714-39.

Nyrop, Richard R., et al., Area Handbook for
Syria.   Washington,   D.C.:   American
University, 1971.

Olson, Robert W., "The Ba'th in Syria 1947-1979: A Interpretative Historical Essay" (Part One), Oriente Moderno, LVIII, No. 12 (December 1978), 645-681' Part Two is in LIX, No. 6 (June 1979), 439-475.

Penrose, Edith and E.R., IRAQ: International Relations and National Development. London: Ernest Benn, 1978.

Peretz, Don, The Middle East Today. New York: Holt, Rhinehart and Winston, 1971 (second edition).

Petran, Tabitha, Syria. New York: Praeger, 1972.

Polk, William R., The United States and the Arab World. Cambridge: Harvard University Press, 1975 (third edition).

_____, The Opening of South Lebanon, 1788-1840: A Study of The Impact of the West on the Middle East. Cambridge: Harvard University Press, 1963.

Quandt, William B., "Political and Military Dimentions of Contemporary Palestinian Nationalism," in The Politics of Palestinian Nationalism, ed., William B. Quandt. Berkeley: University of California Press (1974), 43-154.

Rabinovich, Itamar, Syria Under the Ba'th 1963-66. New York: Halsted Press, 1972.

Sachar, Howard M., Europe Leaves the Middle East 1936-1954, New York: Alfred A. Knopf, 1972.

Safran, Nadav, Israel: The Embattled Ally.
    Cambridge: Harvard University Press, 1978.

Salibi, Kamal S., The Modern History of Lebanon.
    New York: Praeger, 1965.

Schmidt, Dana Adams, Armageddon in the Middle
    East.   New York: The John Day Co., 1974.

Schmucker, Werner.,"Studien zu Ba'th 'Ideologie'"
    (Part I) Die Welt des Islams, XIV/ 14,
    47-80; (Part II). "Der Neobath," XV/ 15,
    (1973), 146-182.

Seale, Patrick, The Struggle for Syria.   London:
    Oxford University Press, 1966.

Sheehan, R.F. Edward, The Arabs, Israelis, and
    Kissinger: A Secret History of American
    Diplomacy in the Middle East, New York:
    Reader's Digest Press, 1976.

Shimon, Shamir, "The Modernization of Syria," in
    William Polk and Richard L. Chambers, eds.,
    Beginning of Modernization in the Middle
    East, the Nineteenth Century, Chicago: The
    University of Chicago Press (1968), 374-75.

Springborg, Robert, "Ba'athism in Practice:
    Agriculture, Politics, and Political Culture in
    Syria and Iraq," Middle Eastern Studies, 17,
    No. 2 (April 1981), 191-209.

Stork, Joe, "Iraq: The War in the Gulf," MERIP
    Reports, No. 97 (June 1981), 3-18.

_____, "Oil and the Penetration of Capitalism
    Iraq: An   Interpretation,"   Peuple
    Mediterraneen   No.   9   (October-December

1979), 125-51.

Tarabishi, Jurj, Sartar wa al-Markisiyah (Sartre Marxism). Dar al-Tali'ah: Beirut, 1974.

Tibawi, A.L., A Modern History of Syria, including Lebanon and Palestine, London, 1969.

Tikriti, Mwafaz, Elites, Administration and Public Policy: A Comparative Study of Republic Regimes in Iraq, 1958-1976. Unpublished Ph.D. thesis University of Texas, 1976.

Torrey, Gordon H., and John F. Devlin, "Arab Socialism," Journal of International Affairs, Vol. XIX, No. 1 (1965), 45-62.

_____, "The Ba'th--Ideology and Practice," Middle East Journal, Vol. XXIII, No. 4 (Autumn 1969), 445-470.

_____, "Instability in Syria," Current History, Vol. 58, no. 341 (January 1970), 13-15, 47-48.

_____, Syrian Politics and the Military, Columbus Ohio: Ohio State University Press, 1964.

Van Dam, Nikolaos, "Middle Eastern Political Cliches: 'Takriti' and 'Sunni Rule' in Iraq; and 'Alawi Rule' in Syria, a Critical Appraisal," Orient, 21, No. 1 (January 1980), 42-57.

_____, "Sectarianism and Regional Factionalism in the Syrian Political Elite," The Middle East Journal, 32 (1978), 201-10.

_____, The Struggle for Power in Syria; Sectarian Regionalism and Tribalism in Politics, 1961-1978. New York: St. Martin's Press, 1979.

Van Dusen, Michael, "Syrian Politics and the Future of Arab-Israeli Relations," in World Politics and the Arab-Israel Conflict (New York: Pergamon Press, 1979), 250-60.

Vatikiotis, P.J., "The Politics of the Fertile Crescent," in Political Dynamics in the Middle East. Paul Y. Hammond and Sidney S. Alexander, eds. New York: American Elsevier (1972), 225-266.

Winder, R. B., "Syrian Deputies and Cabinet Ministers, 1919-1959," Middle East Journal 16(1962),pp. 407-429; 17(1963), pp. 35-54.

Wright, Claudia, "Implications of the Iraq-Iran War; " Foreign Affairs, 59, No. 2 (1980-81), 275-303.

INDEX: THE BA'TH IN SYRIA